THE
SHO' NUFF
PRINCIPLE

THE
SHO' NUFF
PRINCIPLE

A High Achieving Woman's Guide To
Self-Care, Self-Promotion,
& Self-Celebration

DR. LAKILA BOWDEN

Cover design by Revolve Learning
Interior design by Dezign Dogma

Printed in the United States of America
ISBN 9798218747275

First Edition

For permissions or inquiries, contact:
lakila@lakilabowden.com

DISCLAIMER

This book is a work of non-fiction based on the author's personal experiences, opinions, and interpretations. While every effort has been made to present accurate information at the time of writing, the author and publisher make no representations or warranties with respect to the completeness, accuracy, or suitability of the content.

Names and identifying details of individuals, organizations, and events may have been changed, combined, or fictionalized to protect privacy or for narrative clarity. Any similarities to real persons, living or dead, or actual organizations or events are purely coincidental and not intended to represent or malign any individual, group, company, or entity.

The content in this book is intended for informational and inspirational purposes only. It does not constitute legal, medical, psychological, or financial advice. Readers are encouraged to seek professional advice where appropriate.

The author and publisher disclaim any liability for any loss or damage caused or alleged to be caused, directly or indirectly, by the information contained in this book.

For Ma, who would have gotten such a kick out of saying the phrase "Sho' Nuff"!

CONTENTS

INTRODUCTION

The Sho' Nuff Principle

In the first quarter of 2021, two doctors, on two separate occasions, delivered two revelations that would forever change my life.

The first came in February. It was a typical morning. Sunlight streamed through the windows in my master bathroom as I paced the floor, stepping over discarded gym clothes from my earlier workout. Meanwhile, my husband, Eric, was sprawled across our king-size bed, grinning like a Cheshire cat, pumping his fist in the air. His excitement contrasted sharply with my shock as I stared down at four pregnancy tests lined up neatly on the ledge of our garden tub. Two of them boldly displayed plus signs; the others simply said "PREGNANT."

We hadn't been trying. In all my thirty-nine years, I had never been pregnant, and I was convinced my cycle was just running a little late. But a week later, sitting on the exam table in my OB's office, draped in one of those flimsy paper gowns, I got confirmation: pregnancy test number five was accurate. I was five-and-a-half weeks pregnant. Tears filled my eyes, not from fear or confusion, but from sheer joy. Becoming a mom, especially at forty, was the first life-altering revelation.

A few weeks later, the second revelation came, but the setting was much different this time. Instead of looking at sunlight pouring through windows, I was in a sterile exam room lined with old posters harping about A1C levels and barely hanging onto the walls. This time, I wasn't the one wearing the gown. My brave mother, who had been battling cancer for the last three years, sat calmly beside me in the flimsy gown, prattling on about what we'd grab to eat afterward. I, on the other hand, was pacing, unable to focus on food, bracing for news I didn't want to hear.

My worst fears were confirmed when the doctor walked in with that look on her face. "I'm sorry, Mrs. Bowden," she said with a professional empathy that felt rehearsed. "There's nothing else we can do. We'll need to transfer your mother to comfort care and arrange hospice." I understood, but my heart broke. I walked into the hallway, sank to the floor, and cried. I knew, deep down, that my mother wouldn't be there to meet my son, and the weight of that truth crushed me.

I was preparing to become a mother, and I was losing my own mother at the same time. The "superwoman" in me, she could solve everyone's problems in a single bound and stayed ready so she didn't have to get ready, was paralyzed for the first time in my adult life. I drove home in a fog, barely able to see through the tears, and collapsed onto my bed. That night, I sobbed myself to sleep in my husband's arms.

The next morning, I woke up, still overwhelmed by profound joy and deep sorrow but surprisingly rested. I had a new revelation, this was an assignment, one that tested the very core of everything I had ever believed about self-care. Faced with two literal lives on the line, my mother's and my unborn child's, the most important decision I could make was clear: I had to take care of ME.

For the first time in my professional life, in the midst of "life lifing," I pressed pause: no new projects, no revenue-generating ventures, no side hustles. As a retired corporate executive and co-founder of a company, I had always kept my plate full. But this time, I intentionally put everything aside, and my only job became pouring into myself.

During this journey, I realized that to care for my mom in her final days and prepare to welcome my son into the world, I had to prioritize my self-care. I started therapy to navigate the grief I was anticipating. I enlisted the support of local family members and care services to help with my mother's needs. I found an incredible midwife, Mama Sarahn, who mothered me in ways my own mom couldn't at the time. I tapped into a community that helped me prepare for motherhood with grace. I hiked weekly, soaked up natural sunlight, spent intentional time with Eric, laughed as much as possible, and allowed myself to cry when needed.

The people who loved me stepped up, and I let them. I allowed myself to be cared for, and I celebrated every win, big and small. I celebrated how well I cared for my mother, how I created a nurturing womb space for my son, and how I led with light even when a part of the looming outcome was heavy. I spoke to my son daily, in utero, explaining my emotions and welcoming him into my world, full of both joy and sorrow. I practiced non-toxic resilience, asking for help where I needed it and honoring my emotions without falling into the trap of attempting to be "strong" and press on with business as usual.

On July 4, 2021, my beautiful, radiant mother, Jacqueline Renee Bowens, transitioned to the realm of the ancestors. I was six months pregnant when I received the news, right after finishing a hike with my maternal wellness group. Still standing in the parking lot fresh off the trail, my knees buckled, and the only thing keeping me from hitting the ground was Eric's arms. A week later, we threw my mom the ancestral ascension celebration she deserved. Prior to her passing, she made it clear that she didn't want any "sad stuff," so we honored her with a lively homegoing, reflective of her gregarious personality, that people still talk about today.

Three months later, in October, I gave birth to my son, Zaire Aasir. When I saw his face, I cried tears of relief and joy. I had asked my mom to guide him safely into this world, and I felt her presence with me every step of the way.

Because I prioritized my self-care and celebrated my wins, I was able to help my mother live some of her best days in her last days, and my son arrived healthy and joyful. And I, on the other side of it all, thrived, deeply connected to myself, my mother, and my son. After my son's birth, I leaned into redefining rest as my productivity. And so, when I was ready to un-pause and return to running my company, I did so with a renewed sense of clarity. Lucrative projects and ideal clients flowed effortlessly to me, and my business soared. Why? Because I had doubled down on self-care and self-celebration. Through this experience, I developed a cheat code formula that high-achieving women like you can use to create their desired life without burning out.

I've worked with billion-dollar companies like Disney and Kraft Heinz to teach their women leaders how to manage stress and anxiety in the workplace. Now, I'm sharing those cheat codes with you.

I wrote this book to show you that burnout is 100 percent preventable, and to teach you how you can magnetically attract all the things you desire.

You might think, "That's great for you, Lakila, but I don't have a supportive partner or the luxury of resting." You may even be saying to yourself, "Pause?!? Girl, bye!"

Ladies, I hear you. But I'm no different from you. The difference maker and game changer for me and all the women I've coached is applying The Sho' Nuff Principle. The Sho' Nuff Principle says that what you tell yo'self about yo'self will Sho' Nuff become a part of your reality. Knowing this, I developed what I call the "cheat codes" that make for an incredible reality where self-care is prioritized, our wins are celebrated, and we're in a constant state of reward. I call my methods the cheat codes because they're easily accessible. You don't have to go on some Eat, Pray, Love journey to experience the most well-cared-for and highly celebrated version of yourself. Want to get ahead faster and go further while being well-rested and taken care of? Well, this is how you "skip the line," even if your default approach to life has always been to deprioritize your needs.

Long before my mother received a cancer diagnosis, long before my son was even a thought in my mind, and long before I met my husband, I was creating the ideal circumstances for my life by practicing The Sho' Nuff Principle and applying the cheat codes that I'm about to share with you. These principles didn't just come from theory, they came from lived experience, trial and error, and a deep understanding of what it takes to prioritize yourself in a world that keeps asking you to put yourself last.

Having my husband or discretionary income or the luxury of pausing didn't allow me to prioritize my self-care and self-celebration. It was actually the other way around; I had all of those circumstances and the highest quality of them because I prioritized my self-care, self-reward, and self-celebration.

Over the years, my team and I have trained thousands of high-achieving women, and you know what they all had in common? They sucked at self-care and self-celebration. And it wasn't their fault. Like you, they had been conditioned to believe that putting themselves first was selfish, that bragging about their wins was wrong, and that self-care was some luxury to be squeezed in, if time allowed. But it's time to flip the script: self-care, self-reward, and self-celebration are not optional. They are essential.

If you're not sure The Sho' Nuff Principle applies to you (it does), or if you're wondering where to start, I've got you covered. The most important thing is this: start where you are. Don't wait for the "right time," because there's no better time than now. Start by telling yourself you can, even if you don't believe it. Start with the ideal desires for your life in mind without knowing how they'll come to be. Know that you deserve to prioritize your self-care and celebrate yourself, and trust that I'm here to show you exactly how to do it.

Throughout this book, I'll break it down, sharing the steps you need. We'll embark on a transformative journey together. This is not just another self-help book telling you to take bubble baths and journal, although I love a good bubble bath and my journal overfloweth. But to be the most well-cared-for version of yourself, it's essential to understand that self-care is multi-dimensional. We will perfect the art of advocating for ourselves, of mastering the invisible load, and of living with the kind of fulfillment that doesn't require everything in our life to be perfect. Oh, and create a lifestyle that accommodates naps, because who doesn't love a good nap?

In this book, I'm giving you actionable steps to start implementing right now to create the life you desire and move beyond surviving to thriving. The beauty of living in a state of consistent fulfillment is that it's not tied to one specific area of your life being "just right." You can be fulfilled in any moment, in any state, because fulfillment is not about perfection but alignment. It's the foundation of achieving the freedom, abundance, and joy that often seem elusive.

When women put themselves first, everyone and everything in their lives benefits, but most importantly, they benefit. So, sit back, relax, and believe you deserve this. You deserve to live in alignment with who you are, and to magnetically attract the people, resources, and opportunities that are meant for you. By the end of this book, you'll have the keys to making that happen.

Welcome to The Sho' Nuff Principle!

PART ONE

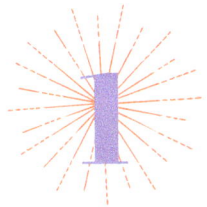

Burnout is 100 Percent Preventable

"Burnout is 100 percent preventable.
Not inevitable."—CJB

Sitting across from me with her usual grace but an unfamiliar weariness, my typically exuberant client Yolanda could not believe the state she found herself in. Between managing a bustling career as a senior VP and her responsibilities as a wife and a mother of three, she felt the pressure consuming her piece by piece. Even her prized cocaine-white Beamer, which had once symbolized her triumphs, seemed to have lost its luster under the weight of exhaustion. The side hustles, the girls' trips, and the late nights spent strategizing her real estate portfolio, all of it had become a foggy blur of achievements that felt empty.

Then there was my client Ava, the youthful, high-powered attorney who once wore the praise of "rising star" like a badge of honor. After leaving corporate law to run her own practice, she found herself juggling the demands of motherhood and a new dream, to open a Play-Care franchise with her husband in her community. But imposter syndrome gnawed at her, feeding on her hesitation. What would her peers say? Would they think she'd lost her mind, chasing something outside the well-defined path of law?

And there was Shante, one of my newer clients, whose resilience and ferocity had earned her a place as the head of a successful government contracting firm. She thrived in the rush of landing multi-million-dollar deals and spearheading a woman-led initiative that shattered industry norms. But beneath the accolades, the invisible load of fifteen-hour workdays, missed workouts, and a body begging for rest was taking its toll. Each attempt to reclaim her fitness led to overexertion, a desperate bid to compensate for lost time, followed by days of immobility. It was a relentless cycle that left her health at the mercy of her ambition.

Two common threads stood out to me when all these women came to me, whether referred by their companies or seeking help on their own. They knew their achievements were monumental, yet they didn't feel accomplished. It turned out that burnout lurked behind their every task, meeting, and interaction. I asked them three questions:

1. What do you do for self-care?
2. How often do you acknowledge the amazing things you've done?
3. How do you celebrate your wins?

Like the hundreds of other women my company either coached or provided corporate training for, all three gave me the same puzzled, deer-in-headlights look like I'd just asked them for my Grandmother Nellie's social security number. These women didn't know each other and had completely different backgrounds, but all were carrying identical brands of baggage: The Invisible Load.

The look in their eyes told me everything. These questions

were foreign, even startling. Their stories, though unique, echoed a kindred common theme. It was the facade of having it all while feeling empty inside for Yolanda. Ava carried the weight of second-guessing herself, paralyzed by what others might think and limiting beliefs around her own lack of experience. Shante battled silently, afraid that admitting she needed rest would crack her painfully built armor. Add to that, they all were the lead parents in their households and the ones in their family and friend groups that everyone tended to lean on.

Their stories were a testament to a silent epidemic among high-achieving women. The pressure to be perfect, prove their worth at every turn, and shoulder everyone else's needs had overshadowed the most important task of all, taking care of themselves.

"Burnout doesn't happen overnight," I explained. "It's a slow build, a steady erosion of joy and energy until you're just a shadow of your once-vibrant self. But the truth is: You don't have to live like that. You can show up and show out, easily, enjoyably, and *well-rested*."

I asked Yolanda, "How do you get so much done at work?"

"Simple," she replied, "I built a rock star team, including my administrative assistant Pamela." Yolanda considered Pamela her right hand on the job.

I then asked Yolanda, "Who is your rockstar team and right hand at home?"

The silence that followed spoke volumes. Yolanda had a husband who shared her load as best he could, but his demanding career left little room for more. The idea of hiring help, nannies, housekeepers, even a chef, felt like admitting defeat.

As I shared with Yolanda how building a "home team" at work had been instrumental to her success, I knew she felt obligated to show up as fiercely for her family, insisting that she handle all tasks that pertained to her children. Her mindset was that if she could achieve so much at work, she should be able to do the same at home.

That's when I shared with Yolanda about my "home team": my nanny, my chef, my housekeeper, even my therapist, all a part of the team that allowed me to thrive in my business but also be fully present with my husband and son *and* get in my coveted naps. As the woman of the household, Yolanda did what all the women in her family had done before her and took the lead on managing the household responsibilities. The thought of a nanny or even a housekeeper seemed like cheating in the face of all they had endured. But when we reframed these helpers as members of the "home team" that kept soul-crushing exhaustion at bay so Yolanda could operate in her gifts and keep her efforts anchored in her zone of genius, she acknowledged that even her Granny would have high-fived her for that. I also explained to Yolanda that the version of the "home team" she crafted could take the shape of whatever was reflective of her needs and current budget. Even freeing up five to ten hours a week could result in a return on investment in time, effort, and income that would have an exponential impact.

Ava's battle with imposter syndrome was not an uncommon challenge to tackle with high-achieving women. She, like many others, had to unlearn the conditioning that kept her tied to pre-dictable, "safe" paths.

Shante needed a new approach, too. She had grown accus-tomed to equating her worth with big efforts, never considering rest as a resolution for some of the biggest challenges she faced.

These women, mirrors of so many others, needed to rewrite the script that said they must sacrifice themselves to succeed. They needed to understand that their light would burn brighter when facing the sun and choosing self-care, self-promotion, and self-celebration as nonnegotiables. They needed to master the invisible load.

What's the Invisible Load?

Many of the women I know, especially the high-achieving ones, carry what I call an invisible load. Yolanda's invisible load looked like appearing to have it all but drowning inside. Ava's invisible load was the fear of failing before even attempting because of impostor syndrome. Shante's invisible load was running a thriving business with failing health but keeping it all to herself. Yours may look like a combination of all three or something altogether different, but you're carrying a load just the same.

It's not only the stuff on your calendar or the work deadlines you must hit. It's the emotional labor, the mental energy, and the pressure of trying to keep it all together. It's the weight of being the perfect mom, the perfect partner, and the perfect boss, while making it look effortless.

And then, on top of that, there's imposter syndrome, pay inequity, and the mental gymnastics we go through just to prove our worth in spaces that don't always recognize it. Add to that the guilt we feel when we even think about putting ourselves first, and you've got a recipe for burnout, and it's kind of like that casserole no one touches at the office potluck. Nobody wants any parts of that...yet it's there, piping hot.

We've been taught to operate on Empty and give from fumes for so long that we don't even realize how much weight we carry. For many of us, martyrdom in womanhood has been glamorized and painted over with a rose-colored film. How many women in your family were praised for being "strong" and holding the family together without the support they needed or at least could have used? This kind of resilience, modeled through generations, held these women captive to unrealistic standards. It is often normalized and adopted as the barometer of our worth and the value we bring to our personal and professional lives. But trust me: Grandma might have done what she had to do, but if the option existed for greater agency over how she was cared for, celebrated, and supported, I'm sure she'd have chosen what the kids today are calling "a soft life."

When the Sh—stuff Hits the Fan!

I want you to take a second and think about whether you've ever had a day, a week, or even a month that was so stressful or made you feel so underappreciated that you thought to yourself, "I've had enough of this sh—stuff."

If you answered yes, you're not alone, and you picked up the right book. I know how it feels because I've been there myself. It's that dreaded space where self-care feels like a myth, where no matter how much you accomplish, it never feels like enough. You check off a thousand tasks, but at the end of the day, you still feel like you've barely scratched the surface.

This is the reality for so many women, especially executives and entrepreneurs like my dear clients Yolanda, Ava, and Shante. We're juggling so many roles, trying to be everything to everyone, except ourselves. We put everyone else first: our teams, our clients, and our families. Meanwhile, we're running on empty, pushing forward from a tank running on fumes, trying to pour from reserves that aren't there. And let me tell you, Friend, that is not sustainable.

The silent epidemic of burnout these women faced was not just theirs, it was ours also. But change was coming, one cheat code at a time, with each decision they made to put themselves first.

You can't be the best version of yourself at home or work when you're constantly operating from a space of depletion. It's a cycle that so many of us fall into, and it's hard to break free from. We've been conditioned to believe that our worth is tied to our productivity, that if we just do more, achieve more, or help more, we'll finally feel fulfilled. Now, I'm sure you've heard the saying, "You can't pour from an empty cup." But truth be told: yes, you most certainly can. I've seen it time and time again, and chances are that if you're reading this book, you are (or a woman you know is) likely an empty cup connoisseur. Although depleted, the reality is that while our cups may be empty of the things we need to show up as our best selves, those of us who are used to over-giving will still find a way to pour into others even if our cups are filled only with air. Did you catch that? We're so conditioned to give, we're giving away our *air*. But consider this: It's not about keeping your cup or bucket full so you have enough to give; it's about treating yourself like a solar panel trained on the sun, powered up so fully that even on cloudy days, you remain fully charged.

Women like us, executives, entrepreneurs, high achievers, are often the worst offenders when it comes to neglecting our own needs. We're so busy trying to handle everything that we forget to take care of ourselves. We forget to face the sun. And the result? Burnout. That creeping, insidious feeling of exhaustion starts taking over every part of your life until you feel lost in your own body and out of touch with your purpose.

The problem is clear. Women are living in a constant state of stress and overwhelm, and it has become such a norm that it's the baseline that has come to define womanhood. Society's expectation is that we focus on everyone else, what they need, what they want, and that we put ourselves at the very bottom of the list. But look at your neighbor and say, "Neighbor, it's a new day, and I'm first!" (If you're alone, look in the mirror and say it.)

In this chapter, we're going to talk about why prioritizing yourself isn't just a nice idea, it's nonnegotiable. We're going to shift the narrative away from burnout, stress, and overwhelm and start focusing on self-care, self-promotion, and self-reward. These aren't luxuries. They are the essential keys to thriving in every area of your life.

This might ruffle some feathers but it's time to stop putting yourself last and start showing up for YOU. Because when you prioritize yourself, everything else rises into alignment with YOUR priority. You'll be more rested, more energized, and, most importantly, fulfilled.

Let me put it out there, ladies. As women, especially high-achieving women, we've been trained to neglect ourselves. At work, at home, in our communities, everyone comes before us. We push, we grind, and we go the extra mile, but at what cost? Burnout is real, and it doesn't just happen because we're tired. It happens because we neglect the most important person in the equation: ourselves.

Here's the great news: Burnout is 100 percent preventable. You get to make choices that don't require you to live on the edge of exhaustion, anxiety, and constant overwhelm. You can reject the standard of conditioning that taking care of yourself, promoting your accomplishments, and rewarding yourself is selfish, unnecessary, or boastful. Allow me to be the battery in your back giving you the boost you need to reframe self-care as your new standard operating procedure, without apology and with all the confidence in the world

Self-care, self-promotion, and self-reward make up the foundation of tangible success that we can feel on the inside and reflect on the outside. They're not indulgences, and they're not afterthoughts once you've taken care of everyone else. They're first. They're foremost. And when you make them nonnegotiable, they're a winning formula.

The Formula: Light In, Light Out

What if we adopted a new barometer where we measure our success based on how full we keep our buckets, how often we rest, and how well our personal and professional relationships pour back into our lives? What if, like that solar panel I mentioned earlier, the expectations of the contributions we emit were anchored in how much light we receive? Instead of burning out, we burn up the invisible loads in our lives with the light of our most whole and healthy versions of ourselves. In this formula, receiving light is the constant multiplying factor, and the math is math-ing in your favor.

Self-Care Is Dynamically Selfless

In those moments of joy and sorrow back in 2021, I had to make a choice. The most important part of that choice wasn't about taking care of my mother or preparing for my son's arrival. The most important decision I made was to take care of myself. Society may try to cast that as a selfish decision when, in fact, it was dynamically selfless. The decision to center myself meant I operated from a state of overflow, which afforded me the capability, grace, and capacity to extend my energy to my mother and son. We, as women, can all stand to benefit from being more self-centered. You must be the top priority in your own life.

Whether it's booking time with your therapist, building your "home team," carving out space for meditation, or simply allowing yourself to take a nap, whatever acts of self-care resonate with you and what you need at the moment, do it. When you're filled up, everything else flows from that place. You show up better at work, with your family, and in every area of your life. But we can't talk about self-care, self-promotion, or even celebration without addressing the most important aspect: self-centering your mental and emotional well-being. Get your mind right, and the desires of your heart will follow.

We live in a world that pushes us to our limits, glorifies over-working, and celebrates the grind, but that grind can grind you down to a nub. While convincing us that our productivity is tied to our worth, the world we live in constantly calls our "enough-ness" into question.

Burnout is real but preventable. Anxiety, stress, and emo-tional exhaustion are real but preventable. The way we combat them is by making a conscious decision to stack the deck in our favor by prioritizing our mental and emotional health rather than making it an afterthought.

The Silent Epidemic of Burnout

The scariest part about burnout is that it often creeps up on you slowly. As we've already learned from Yolanda, Ava, and Shante, you don't necessarily just wake up one day feeling burnt out, it builds over time. One moment, you're managing, and the next, a string of days have passed where it feels like everything is just too much. That's why it's so important to start taking care of your mental and emotional well-being long before you get to that breaking point.

If you've ever questioned whether it's just you, it's not: *high-achieving women are especially vulnerable to burnout.* Why? Because societal expectations and conditioning has us always going, always doing, always pushing ourselves to the limit. We take on more responsibilities at work, at home, and in our personal lives. We're not just juggling one ball, we're juggling a dozen balls while also directing an entire circus, herding a ring of cats, and balancing on a freaking unicycle! And even when we're exhausted, we keep going because we've been taught so well that we do it on autopilot. We automatically give away the air in our "empty cup" without a second thought.

To be clear, it ain't cute. It's not reasonable. And it sure isn't sustainable. The cost of showing up for everyone else and neglecting yourself is too damn high. It's time to start prioritizing your mental and emotional health, every single day that ends in *y*, and not just when you've done something to deserve it, but because you *exist*. Put yourself first when it feels uncomfortable, without the answers to what everyone else is going to do, without you putting them first, and *before* you put somebody in a full-on chokehold. (Don't act like I'm the only one who's been tempted to go full WrestleMania on the next person who asks for my help for the fifty-eleventh time.)

Burnout Isn't Just Physical

When we talk about burnout, most people think of physical exhaustion, but that's only one aspect. Burnout is insidious, and its tentacles burrow in and cause emotional, mental, and spiritual exhaustion, too. It's that feeling of waking up every day and wondering why you're even doing all of this. It's pushing through the motions but feeling disconnected from the work you're doing. It's looking around at everything you've accomplished and still feeling like it's not enough.

Burnout sneaks up on you when you've neglected yourself for too long. It's like a slow drain, a leaky faucet in the background that you don't notice until one day you realize you're completely tapped out.

As my client Shante recounted to me her vicious cycle of working long stretches of fifteen-hour days, finally having a morning with enough time to cram in a workout only to go too hard in the gym and end up racked with pain, I pointed out to her that it was as if she was punishing herself. She'd never considered that physically taking care of herself included rest. Replacing her bouts of strenuous exercise with gentle yoga and a steady-state walk could accomplish not only her goal of physical fitness but also provide the mental and emotional relief she needed to decompress from her long workdays without requiring huge exertions of energy she really didn't have.

In addition to revamping Shante's approach to physical wellness, we also addressed her personal celebration and reward system, or lack thereof. Shante had done what only 2 percent of women-owned businesses had been able to accomplish, generating over $1M in revenue annually in her business. But never once in the many years that she'd been accomplishing this incredible feat, year after year, had she ever taken the time to really acknowledge it. I shot her a look and said, "You're killing it, but your celebration game's gotta improve, ASAP!"

With a plan in place to celebrate her wins and redirect her physical fitness efforts, Shante did a one-eighty in just under four months. Walking daily, being more thoughtful about her food choices, and getting some sleep allowed her to release over twenty pounds, giving her a ton more energy. Her personal celebration plans, which now included visits to her favorite local bookstore to sip her favorite rooibos chai tea, Sunday morning hikes, and investing in private salsa lessons so she could shake a tailfeather on her upcoming trip to Latin America, genuinely began to infuse real joy into her journey because she had her thoughtful mini-celebrations to look forward to on the regular.

That's why giving yourself permission to prioritize self-care and self-celebration is so important. It's the antidote to burnout.

When you give yourself permission to rest, to ask for what you need, and to celebrate your wins, you're facing the sun, keeping your solar panel charged and maintaining reserves in the tank. You're making sure that burnout never gets a chance to slide into your DMs.

The Signs of Burnout

Before we dive into how to take care of your mental and emotional well-being, let's talk about the warning signs of burnout. If you can recognize these signs early, you can start taking steps to prevent them from getting worse. Here are some key things to look out for:

1. **Emotional exhaustion:** You're not just tired, you're energetically drained. You feel like you have nothing left to give, and even small tasks feel overwhelming.
2. **Detachment:** You feel disconnected from your work, your relationships, or even yourself. You're going through the motions, but you don't feel fully present or engaged in anything.
3. **Lack of motivation:** The things that used to excite or motivate you no longer bring you joy. You've lost interest in things you used to love and find it hard to muster up the energy to care.
4. **Irritability or mood swings:** You're more irritable than usual, and small things set you off. You find yourself snapping at people or feeling emotionally volatile.
5. **Physical symptoms:** Burnout isn't just mental; it's physical, too. You might experience headaches, insomnia, muscle tension, or even more serious health issues as a result of prolonged stress.

In a nutshell, you're "over it"...whatever *it* is. If any of these signs sound familiar, it's time to take action. I'll also point out that you may find that you're not experiencing any of these signs per se, but when you pause to think about the last time you did something just for yourself, truly celebrated even a minor milestone, gave yourself props for a job well-done, nothing comes to mind. That means you're on the slippery slope to burnout town. Don't wait until you hit rock bottom to start prioritizing your mental and emotional health. In the case of burnout, an ounce of prevention is worth a pound of cure.

The Main Thing

Here's the main thing about the main thing: High-achieving women like you, juggling careers, family, and endless to-do lists, often prioritize everything and everyone else while running on fumes. But prioritizing yourself isn't selfish, it's dynamically selfless and essential for living a fulfilling, balanced life. Self-care, self-promotion, and self-celebration aren't just nice-to-haves; they're the foundations for thriving rather than merely surviving. Embracing that it's okay to put yourself first is the first step toward escaping the cycle of burnout and stress. You deserve to show up as not just your best self but the most well-cared-for and celebrated version of yourself in every part of your life, and that can only happen when you commit to taking care of yourself. This is your wake-up call to recognize that success doesn't have to come at the expense of your well-being. By shifting your mindset, granting yourself permission, and embracing self-care unapologetically, you can break the cycle and live a life that's both accomplished and fulfilling.

As we move forward in this book, keep in mind that prioritizing yourself isn't just important; it's necessary. It's time to give yourself the grace, care, and celebration you truly deserve.

Takeaways:

1. **Be a solar panel, not an empty cup connoisseur.** You actually *can* pour from an empty cup, giving away your air, but at what cost? Lean toward "the sun", the things, people, and mind food that keep you charged up and energized. If you decide to give, pull that energy from your overflow. Prioritizing yourself is paramount to fulfillment.

2. **Stress and overwhelm ain't cute or sustainable.** True success isn't solely defined by professional achievements. It comes from embracing self-care and self-celebration as your standard operating procedure of professional and personal fulfillment.

3. **Self-care is dynamically selfless.** Prioritizing self-care, self-promotion, and self-reward is how we curate and nurture the best version of ourselves, you benefit, and so does everyone and everything else.

4. **Unapologetically prioritize you.** When you take care of yourself first, your work, relationships, and personal well-being rise in alignment with your priority.

Our Power Is in Our Own Permission

"I've accomplished so much, so why don't I feel accomplished?"—LJB

My client, Yolanda, sat at her desk, surrounded by the symbols of her success, framed degrees, awards, and photographs from corporate events where she was celebrated. Yet the weight in her chest told a different story. No matter how many promotions she achieved or milestones she crossed, she couldn't shake the feeling she was running on empty. The sparkle in her eyes that once mirrored her ambition had dulled, replaced by a silent question she couldn't answer: Why do I feel so incomplete? In one of our coaching sessions, she finally built up the nerve to ask me this question out loud. I looked at her with deep, knowing empathy and said, "Because you're last on your list and waiting for permission that you already possess."

Women who are high achievers are taught to keep pushing, keep grinding, and keep achieving. And that becomes a double-edged sword where we amass incredible accomplishments and continue pushing the goalpost further and further away. I've been there. You've got the degrees, the promotions, the accolades. On paper, it looks like you've made it. But deep down, something's missing. You've done all the things, checked all the boxes, and yet, there's still that nagging feeling like you're not quite there. You're running things, even if you're exhausted, and despite all your achievements, you feel unfulfilled or less fulfilled than you should. I hear you. And I know that pressure all too well.

To be clear, your accomplishments matter. Your drive to set a goal, accomplish it, and still strive for more is magnificent and something to celebrate. At the same time, no external success can fill the void if you're not aligned with your inner needs. If you haven't given yourself permission to prioritize you, you'll always feel like something's missing.

The number one reason my women clients tell me they don't prioritize themselves is that they feel an overwhelming sense of guilt. That's right. When women attempt to prioritize our self-care over our careers and over the families we lead and love, we feel *guilty*. And it's not our fault. We legitimately live in a society that has adopted what I call the Flawed Hierarchy of Expectations for Women's Priorities. At the top is everyone else, followed by everything else, and then somewhere around the bottom, there's you. And, of course, this hierarchy benefits everyone and everything else, but you, not so much. Let me encourage you to boldly rearrange the order of priorities. I want you to put YOU at the top of the list.

Society's Hierarchy of Priorities for Women

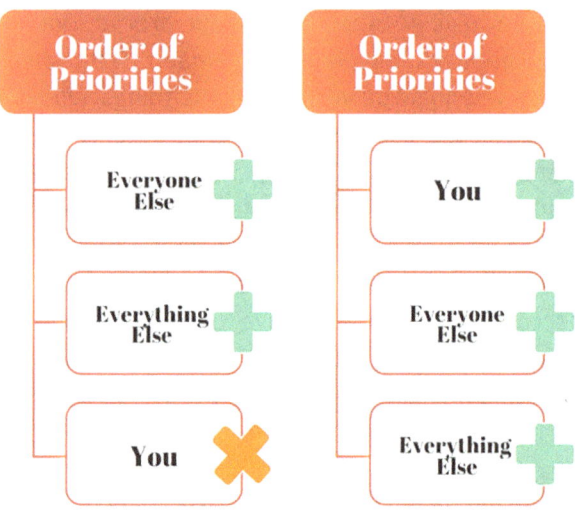

Now, for those out there who may be saying, "Well, Lakila, what about everyone else, and what about everything else?!" Whoever's saying that can cool their jets. The truth is that when you rearrange the order and put yourself first, everyone else and everything else continues to benefit, and so do you!

You see, ladies, giving yourself permission to prioritize self-care and celebrate yourself is the superpower that lifts the invisible loads in your lives.

Our power is in our own permission, and let's not forget that we teach others how to treat us based on how we treat ourselves. The power of our own permission is the accomplishment that makes us feel accomplished.

Tina's Teacup

Once upon a time in my corporate career, I worked alongside a director colleague, Tina. Tina was a retired Naval Officer turned corporate rockstar. During her tenure in the military, she'd earned all the medals, all the respect, and all the credentials. Tina was able to transition into leadership in corporate America and maintain that same level of respect and regard for her abilities. She was a talented leader, often called upon for her strategic expertise, but it wasn't simply her hard work that garnered admiration from peers, colleagues, and more senior executives alike. As I observed Tina, I understood why her presence elicited such an admirable response.

One day, during an all-day quarterly team meeting, I noticed all the other leaders bustling into the room, frantically prepping to report on their region's metrics, with coffee in plain white disposable cups. I then glanced over at Tina and saw that Tina was not drinking coffee; Tina was drinking tea. As if she had no care in the world, Tina was casually sipping her tea from a real teacup, yes, a fancy porcelain teacup, complete with a tiny stirrer spoon and saucer to boot. In fact, I realized Tina was having her own personal "tea party" right in the midst of our leadership meeting. It became part of her ritual, part of her self-care practice. She would sit down at the table, pour herself a cup of tea, and sip it slowly while the meeting carried on. It reminded her that she was in control of her time, energy, and peace.

My takeaway from watching Tina and her teacup over time was that Tina was held in high regard and treated with respect because of how she treated herself. She taught the people around her how to treat her by showing them that she valued herself and her time. That teacup became a symbol of her power, a daily reminder that she was giving herself permission to prioritize her own needs in the midst of all the chaos.

Tina and her teacup are the perfect example of what I'm talking about when I say you must give yourself permission. You have to set the boundaries, create the rituals, and make the decisions that put you first, no matter what anyone else thinks. (Let the haters hate.) That's how you operate from a place of power.

Tina's story resonated deeply with Yolanda when I shared it. The idea that self-care could be woven into the fabric of daily life, even amidst the chaos of work, was foreign to her. She often wondered what it would look like to claim those small, sacred moments without feeling like she was taking away from her family or career. The idea simmered in her mind, sparking a vision of what her own version of "teatime" might be, a ritual that gave her a breath of peace during her whirlwind days. I had revealed what Yolanda needed to start feeling complete.

As we continued our coaching sessions, the idea of giving herself permission lingered in Yolanda's mind. It was an unfamiliar concept, like an uncharted territory she had avoided. Permission, I explained, wasn't just about taking a break; it was about breaking the silent contract she'd made with herself, the one that said she had to earn her rest, earn her peace, and earn the right to pause to acknowledge her incredible accomplishments along the path of her career journey. The weight of that realization settled over her, both intimidating and freeing.

This was when I introduced Yolanda to the Permission to Power Pyramid, a framework I've developed to guide clients on tapping into the full breadth of their internal power and showing up as the best version of themselves in all spaces. I'm sharing it here now with you so you, too, can tap in.

The Permission to Power Pyramid: Solid as a Rock

The Permission to Power Pyramid is your roadmap to self-care, self-promotion, and self-reward, supporting you in consistently

Permission to Power Pyramid

walking in your power. The Permission to Power Pyramid is built on this concept. At the foundation, you give yourself permission to prioritize your self-care, which incites a snowball effect that goes from permission to practice to peace to power.

Now, here is a quick note on the term *permission*. The base of the framework is permission, and that's very intentional. I know the word "permission" can be charged for my go-getters. I am a woman who thrives in the "forgiveness over permission" lane. I do a thing I want to do, and it'll be done long before I mess around asking for permission. I'm not the type to ask timidly if I can do what needs to be done while avoiding eye contact and wringing my hands. I've found that "asking for permission" is often unnecessary and can open up the possibility of what I want being withheld. But that applies strictly to external permission. When it comes to me internally, I don't hesitate to give myself permission to pursue the things that spark joy in my life, invite peace and calm, or serve me best. The permission I'm referencing in the Permission to Power Pyramid framework is your own internal permission. It's the only permission you need to act in your own best interest. It's essential and fundamental, so it's where we start in this framework. It is, in fact, your own permission that spearheads alleviating the guilt we often feel when considering putting our needs first. Your own permission gets your needs off the back burner and to the top of the priority list. With the guilt gone, we're already one massive invisible load lighter.

Yolanda, looked at the pyramid and felt a pang of recognition. She had spent her life asking others, her boss, her peers, even her family, for validation, never realizing that the permission she needed most had to come from within. The concept of building her life on her own terms, without the need for external approval, was revolutionary. It felt like someone had opened a door she didn't know existed.

Each level of the pyramid builds on the one before it, creating a solid foundation that supports and empowers you to show up as the most well-cared-for version of yourself. Let's break down each level and how it all comes together to create a life where you thrive instead of just survive the day.

We've established that the first step is you internally granting yourself permission. After we've given ourselves permission to prioritize self-care, we're primed to successfully engage in becoming consistent in the next level of the pyramid, which is the practice of self-care. Allow me to point out here that practicing self-care doesn't require sweeping change. In fact, attempting sweeping change will fail you, and it's likely why you don't *self-care* and *self-reward* today. The thought of drinking all the water, getting all the sleep, racking up retail therapy, getting your hair and nails done, and waking up at five in the morning to meditate before being a super mom, wife, and BFF is already exhausting. Oh, and don't forget to hit the gym and travel for leisure!

Pump the brakes; practicing self-care is not about overcrowding your already overcrowded to-do list. When instituting self-care practices, we simply want to Take Two. Identify two of the simplest self-care practices you can access right now and start with those. When it comes to practicing self-care, we want to be consistent and successful. We set ourselves up for failure when we try to do everything at once. Even if we start out strong, eventually it becomes too much, doesn't work with our schedule, or we just get plain old sick of trying to be "perfect." However, when we apply the concept of Take Two, we get good and consistent at two things that eventually become our default self-care practices. Then, we can Take Two with another set of self-care practices and build from there. I recommend Taking Two for at least ninety days before adding another set of practices. We live in a microwave world where it feels like everything has to happen overnight and fast, fast, fast, but we're talking about lasting and sustainable change. So, invest the ninety days and give yourself the gift of Take Two instead of trying to take in everything. It's the difference between boiling a pot of water and trying to boil the ocean.

So now we've got permission poppin' off and practice crackin'. When we're working from this rock-solid foundation of permission and consistent practice, it activates our peace, internally and externally. Peace looks like a nervous system that knows how to regulate itself when overstimulated. Peace looks like a mind that focuses on solutions and opportunities and doesn't spiral down a rabbit hole of horrible, unlikely outcomes. Peace looks like expectations of everything working out in our favor without knowing exactly *how* it will work out. When we're faced with all that sh—stuff we talked about earlier, the imposter syndrome, the pay inequity, imbalanced household workloads, and the various other invisible loads in our lives, we can navigate from a place of peace of mind. And *that* is where our power lies: at the top of the pyramid!

Our true power is rooted in a deeply ingrained ability to trust our own intuition, and it's reaffirmed and strengthened every time we pour into ourselves. Our power is an energy that someone can feel and that elicits support and favor without exorbitant effort on our part, meaning you don't have to be doing the most, ladies. Our power often speaks for itself before we enter a room or utter a word.

When we go from permission to practice to peace to power, we're empowered to ask for more money or raise our prices. We're empowered to select work environments that align with our values. We're empowered to kick imposter syndrome to the curb and know we're enough. We're empowered to make choices that serve us best without giving it a second thought.

When you consistently give yourself permission, practice self-care, and operate from a place of peace, you tap into your full power. You become more productive, creative, and aligned with your purpose. Productivity includes rest, by the way. So, as you continue your journey, remember: give yourself permission, Take Two, start with small, consistent practices, embrace the peace that comes from prioritizing yourself, and step fully into your power.

The Main Thing

Here's the main thing about the main thing: You've accomplished so much, and you're more than enough. But if you want to eradicate your invisible loads, if you want to feel fulfilled, if you're going to avoid burnout, you have to start giving yourself permission to take care of *you*.

The Permission to Power Pyramid is how you access and leverage the full extent of your power that's generated by prioritizing your needs. It's rooted in knowing that your worth doesn't require proof. You were born worthy. It's time to own that.

In the next chapter, we'll dive deeper into my personal self-care cheat codes that you can easily incorporate into your own self-care practice. But for now, I want you to take a moment and ask yourself: "What do I need to give myself permission to do today?" Whether it's taking a break, asking for help, or celebrating something you've achieved, whatever it is, give yourself that permission. The power that comes with your own permission is exactly the power you need to show up in the world as the badass that you really are inside and out! Sho' Nuff.

Takeaways:

1. **Stand on your own permission.** Grant yourself the permission to prioritize and celebrate yourself without guilt. Your own permission is all the go ahead you need.

2. **Take two.** Self-care and self-celebration don't require sweeping changes. Start with two small, intentional actions that have a big impact and keep at it for at least ninety days. Then, Take Two more actions to work on. Before you know it, you're living in a constant state of self-care and self-celebration badassery!

3. **Practice is the path to peace.** Consistent practice of self-care and self-celebration give you peace of mind, which shows up in your body and the energy you emit, and permeates your internal thoughts and external actions. Operating from a place of peace is how we position ourselves to alleviate stress and underappreciation, living in alignment with practices that support our own fulfillment.

4. **Exude your power.** Tapping into your power clears the path for you, activating your intuition and attracting resources and opportunities that fill you up instead of draining you. A woman who deeply knows her own power and actively taps into it becomes limitless.

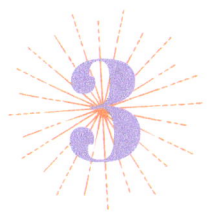

Cheat Code One: Exercise Self-Compassion

"Beating yourself up over almost anything is a waste of time." —LJB

Start with Positive Self-Talk

Let's talk about your most important relationship, the one you have with yourself. How do you speak to yourself on a daily basis? When things go wrong, or you don't meet that impossible standard you've set, what's the first thing you say in your head? Are you kind? Are you patient? Or are you quick to criticize and tear yourself down?

Ava fought this battle all too often as she continued volleying the thought of pivoting from a well-established legal career into what some would consider a passion project. To make matters worse, every time a project at work didn't go perfectly, the voice in her head would echo accusations: "You should have seen that coming. How could you mess that up? This is why you shouldn't be an entrepreneur." She would replay each misstep as if reviewing a court transcript, picking apart every detail and blaming herself relentlessly. This constant loop of self-criticism chipped away at her confidence, making even the smallest mistakes feel monumental.

The reality is that most of us are a lot harder on ourselves than we'd ever be on anyone else. We'll give grace to our friends, family, colleagues, and even strangers, but when it comes to our own slip-ups or shortcomings, we're mercilessly unforgiving. That's where self-compassion comes in. It's the first cheat code I'm sharing with you, because exercising self-compassion is within your full control. It's the foundation of The Sho' Nuff Principle.

Studies have shown a significant correlation between stress and anxiety being lower in positive self-talkers, resulting from reduced cortisol levels. That's excellent news, because it means we can use our internal dialogue to manage what's going on inside our bodies and minds. The Sho' Nuff Principle, remember, what you tell yo'self about yo'self will *sho' nuff* become a part of your reality, means that choosing to commit to positive self-talk and a healthy inner dialogue positions us for more fulfilling experiences and greater confidence in our decisions and pursuits.

Self-Compassion and Grace

Here's the part where we need to have a real talk about grace. Most of us are ridiculously hard on ourselves, constantly raising the bar and expecting perfection in everything we do. I can't tell you how many times I've heard women say and really mean that they're their own worst critics, picking apart every little mistake, missed deadline, and moment where they didn't meet an impossibly high self, or society-imposed standard. But where's the grace?

For Ava, the lack of grace was evident in how she dissected her work after every trial. Even when she won a case, her mind raced to the one argument she could have presented better, the one sentence she should have said differently. The self-imposed pressure followed her home, where she found it difficult to relax, haunted by a nagging sense of inadequacy despite her success. That sense of inadequacy made her question whether she was fit to even consider a venture outside the law, and it made her forget that before she made her success in her legal career, she began as an eager novice in law. In our coaching sessions, I helped her embrace the idea that she could use her internal dialogue to remind herself about herself, and that her skillset and gumption to try had already amassed significant success in her current legal career and were indeed transferrable to whatever future venture she decided to pursue.

Exercising self-compassion means extending to yourself real and actionable grace. Yes, you're human. Yes, you'll have off days. We all inherently understand that perfection is impossible, yet our measure for success is often anchored in perfection. So, when I say exercise self-compassion and real grace, I mean even when you feel you're flat-out failing, continue to celebrate yourself for making an effort. Allow yourself to attempt things and embrace unintended or unwanted outcomes as a critical part of the learning process. When you win or knock something out of the park, celebrate it like you won a championship ring. I mean, pop a bottle or something!

Acknowledging that you're human means remembering that progress in an area counts for something when you're doing the best you can with what you've got, and that's something to celebrate, not criticize.

We tend to be so compassionate with everyone else in our lives, our partners, our kids, our coworkers, while carelessly denying ourselves an inkling of the same understanding. It's time to cut the criticism. You deserve the same kindness, compassion, and forgiveness you extend to others. Give yourself permission to fly. And give yourself permission to fall short. And use the voice in your head to remind yourself that you're the bomb every day that ends in *y*.

Exercising Self-Compassion for the Win: Lavonda's Fortunate Error

This was certainly the case for Lavonda, a client of mine whose IT firm won a huge contract. Lavonda was initially a negative self-talker and constantly beat herself up for any little error. Well, after weeks of working with my team on focusing on positive self-talk, one day, her team made an error in reporting that truly pissed off her client. Lavonda normally would have gone down a rabbit hole of self-loathing, which would likely have caused the client to lose trust in her ability. Instead, she owned the mistake and developed a plan that not only resolved the issue but brought a whole new value proposition to the table.

As fate would have it, when Lavonda presented her solution to the contracting team, she was told it was too late and they were moving on with another vendor. Lavonda said she understood, took great pride in her solution, and offered her support if ever the opportunity arose in the future. Later that night, Lavonda took her team out for drinks to celebrate their efforts and the lessons learned from the situation. A month later, one of the internal stakeholders from her previous client who'd joined a new agency reached out to offer an even bigger contract to Lavonda. He explained that he'd been in the meeting that day when she kept her cool and presented what he thought was a brilliant reconciliation plan. He was impressed with her accountability and quick, confident solution. The fact that she wasn't overly apologetic and hadn't tucked her tail and run let him know he could trust her work.

I asked Lavonda what was going through her head at the moment she lost the initial contract, which led to her response and later celebrating with her team. She said to me, "Lakila, I thought about our coaching convos, and I kept repeating to myself, "I'm good at what I do. One mistake does not degrade my impeccable talent. And I moved forward with that energy."

Lavonda took my guidance to go on a hunt for the lessons instead of the losses, and she began to see opportunities she would have otherwise missed. Regularly applying this level of self-compassion fueled an acceleration in her wins, and most importantly, she released that beat-up feeling and replaced it with a bolder, more confident, and more decisive energy.

In my coaching with Lavonda, I emphasized a core tenet of The Sho' Nuff Principle: Always tell yourself that the outcome will be in your favor and better than you expect. Sometimes, you have an outcome in mind, and you're so anchored to it that if it doesn't come to pass, you feel demoralized. With the wind knocked out of your sails, it's hard to recover, let alone feel prepared to get back on your feet. But applying The Sho' Nuff Principle and telling ourselves everything will work out in our favor or better than expected opens up a world of possibilities. Whether the specific thing you're seeking happens or not becomes irrelevant to receiving an even more favorable experience.

My own first multi-million-dollar commercial contract came while pursuing a coveted government contract that I ultimately did not win. But, because I was so open to the power of positive possibilities, I treated the "denial" as a delay with no bearing on my worthiness. I continued operating with confident energy that led to my developing a relationship along the journey which eventually opened doors I didn't initially realize existed, propelling my company to a new stratosphere of financial success.

Why Positive Self-Talk Matters

Real quick, let me point out that, the doors of The Sho' Nuff Principle swing in two directions, because what you tell yourself about yourself becomes your reality. If you're constantly feeding your mind with negativity, "I'm not good enough," "I'm not smart enough," "I'm a failure", then that's exactly what you'll believe. And when you believe that, you start showing up in the world with that energy. You start playing small, holding back, and second-guessing yourself.

But everything changes when you flip the script and start talking to yourself like your own best friend. Positive self-talk doesn't mean ignoring reality or pretending everything is perfect. It means choosing to speak to yourself in a way that builds you up instead of tearing you down.

I invite you to try this out during your workweek. Whenever doubt creeps in, counter it with, "I'm capable, and I've got this, and if I don't got it, I'm-a get it." At first, it may feel awkward, almost forced, but keep it up and you'll observe a subtle shift. The internal dialogue that was once stifling will begin to inspire, allowing you room to breathe and trust yourself.

The Power of Self-Compassion

Exercising self-compassion isn't just a nice idea, it's a powerful tool that can transform how you show up in your life and work. When you regularly practice self-compassion, you give yourself the space to make mistakes, to learn, and to grow without the crushing weight of guilt or shame. You free yourself from the need for perfection and open up to the possibility of progress.

Holding guilt over past mistakes doesn't make women better leaders, wives, mothers, colleagues, or friends. In fact, it does the opposite while also making us more anxious and less effective. The moment you start to show yourself the same grace you give others, your confidence grows, and you become a more powerful presence, both at work and at home.

How to Start Exercising Self-Compassion

So, how do you actually start exercising self-compassion? It begins with awareness, becoming mindful of the way you speak to yourself and consciously choosing to shift that inner dialogue. Here are a few ways you can get started:

Reframe negative thoughts. Whenever you feel the familiar rise of self-criticism, or the next time you catch yourself in a spiral of negative self-talk, pause and ask yourself: "Would I speak this way to a friend?" If the answer is no, then you shouldn't be saying it to yourself either. Take that negative thought and reframe it into something more compassionate. For example, instead of "I'll never get this right," try "This is challenging, but I'm learning, and I'm proud of myself for trying."

Give yourself grace. We all make mistakes, but beating yourself up over them doesn't help. When you slip up, practice giving yourself the same grace you'd offer someone else. Remind yourself that you're human, and humans aren't perfect. Learn from the mistake and literally let it go without dwelling on it. Time spent ruminating on mistakes is incredibly wasteful and detracts from the value you could be contributing to a situation or even the rest you could be catching up on.

Celebrate small wins. We'll talk about this more in Chapter Six, but self-compassion isn't just about being kind to yourself when things go wrong, it's also about celebrating when things go right. Take time to acknowledge your efforts, no matter how small. Did you finish that task you've been putting off? Celebrate it. Did you make it through a tough day at work? Celebrate that, too. These small moments of celebration build a foundation of self-compassion and remind you that you're doing a great job, even when it feels like you're just getting by. So, give yourself big props on the regular.

The Sho' Nuff Principle in Action

The Sho' Nuff Principle is a powerful method of showing up in your life with confidence, resilience, and joy, and it starts with exercising self-compassion through positive self-talk, extending grace to ourselves, and treating our losses as lessons. You have to speak power over yourself and know that you are worthy of every good thing that comes your way.

Exercising self-compassion is the magic in your superpower toolkit, it's the secret sauce that you and you alone have full control over. Without it, you'll keep running yourself into the ground, chasing perfection, and never feeling like you're enough. But when you start exercising self-compassion, you open the door to a new way of living, one where you show up for yourself first, celebrate your wins, and trust that no matter what, you've got your own back.

The Main Thing

Here's the main thing about the main thing: Exercising self-compassion is the first cheat code because it's fully within your own control. If you want to build a thriving life, a successful career, and healthy relationships, then take a hard pass on ever beating yourself up and spend the large majority of your energy *building* yourself up. We're solar panels, remember, and your internal dialogue is a part of the sunlight that keeps you charged. It's time to start speaking kindly to yourself, giving yourself grace, and celebrating all that you are and all that you've achieved.

In the next chapter, we'll talk about mindfulness and how being fully present in your life can help you manage stress, ignite your intuition, and live with intention. But for now, I want you to start exercising self-compassion. Pay attention to the way you speak to yourself. When those negative thoughts creep in, simply cut them off, remembering you deserve kindness, grace, and compassion just as much as anyone else. Let the voice in your head be that of the kindest chick you know.

Takeaways:

1. **Whatever you say to yourself, remember you're always listening.** Our internal dialogue becomes our thoughts, and our thoughts drive our dominant energy and actions. You can use positive self-talk to alleviate stress and anxiety while still holding yourself accountable and showing up as the most well-cared-for version of yourself.

2. **Prioritize grace over perfection.** Treat your wins as inevitable and your losses as lessons. Accept that you will make mistakes, and give yourself grace in the process. Perfection isn't the goal, progress is.

3. **Self-compassion reduces stress.** Your body and emotional state respond positively to positive self-talk. By being kind to yourself, you ease stress, anxiety, and pressure to always be perfect.

4. **Unlock your potential with compassion.** Exercising self-compassion can unlock access to the solutions, oppor-

tunities, and relationships needed to reach the next level of your career and personal life. Being compassionate with yourself maximizes your internal and external value and minimizes your blind spots.

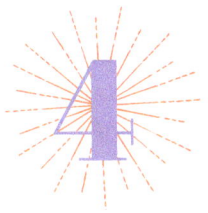

Cheat Code Two: Activate Mindfulness

"This is mindfulness for the busy 'brain-did.'"—LJB

Being Fully Present Through Intention, Breathing, and Movement

Straight up, I have a busy brain, and if you're anything like me, your brain is always going, going, going too. I call that being busy "brain-did." Between work deadlines, family obligations, and the constant pressure to be "on" all the time, being busy can leave you exhausted and mentally drained. Yet your mind is still off to the races. That's where mindfulness comes in.

Mindfulness is defined as the act of being fully present. Your mental presence is what helps to stave off stress and anxiety triggers. Presence allows us to enjoy the moments in our lives versus going on autopilot and missing the good parts, including the sticky, icky parts. Presence invites calm, confidence, and connection with ourselves and the people around us. This cheat code isn't just about slowing down for the sake of it, it's about learning to activate our ability to be fully in the moment and fully present for all the parts that make life worth living. Activating mindfulness is the difference between feeling like life is rushing past you and feeling like you're in the driver's seat, steering with intention.

As a high-achieving woman, you probably know this feeling well. Have you ever caught yourself moving through the day on autopilot, shuffling between conference calls, project deadlines, and dinner prep without pausing to take a breath? And you realize that every last word spoken by the person in front of you for the past ten minutes sounds eerily similar to the teacher's voice in *Charlie Brown*, "whomp-whomp-whomp-whomp-whomp", and you can't recall a thing you've just discussed. That realization can be especially sobering when the voice across from you comes from someone you truly love, like your child, spouse, or best friend. You're mortified to think of how many moments you may have missed and how few chances you may have left before the people on the other side check out on you, opting instead for the company or listening ear of those who make them feel acknowledged.

Don't worry; all is not lost for you, my busy, brain-did friend. Even with full plates, we can still activate mindfulness, my second self-care cheat code, and we can do it with intention, breathing, and movement.

Mindfulness Fuels Our Intuition

Let's strip mindfulness down to its simplest form: it's about being present on purpose. It's about paying attention to what's happening right now instead of getting lost in the past or too wrapped up in the future to appreciate the present. It's about tuning in to your body, your breath, your thoughts, and your emotions without judgment, just noticing them for what they are.

We live in a world that rewards multitasking and constant productivity. But in reality, doing more isn't always the answer. Sometimes, the most powerful thing you can do is the simplest thing you can do. When activating mindfulness, the simple things are to intend, breathe, and move. That's where real clarity comes from. That's where you can start to truly hear your intuition and make decisions from a place of calm instead of chaos.

Activating mindfulness allows us to tap into our intuitive capabilities. Every woman was born with intuition, that sixth sense that lets you know something is off, like maybe you need to check your boyfriend's phone, or that tells you everything is A-okay and that an opportunity you've been considering is a perfect fit for you!

We're born with intuition. You don't have to purchase it; you simply have to tap into it. When we activate mindfulness, we can eliminate much of the stress that comes from bickering with our intuition. In fact, remaining in a state of stress will only lead you to blatantly act in opposition to your intuition.

Acting in opposition to our intuition may look like the relationship we stay in too long, even though we know things aren't quite right. It may look like making choices on the job to get along, even though it really grates on our soul. It's the number of times we say, "I knew from the jump this wasn't gonna work," after doing the thing anyway.

Your intuition is a muscle that can be strengthened, no matter how weak or quiet it has become. The quiet and weak intuitive muscle is far from harmless, by the way. It's compounding your guilt about attempting to prioritize yourself, exacerbating your stress response and feeding toxic resilience.

But when we activate mindfulness, we also activate and strengthen our intuitive capabilities, improving their accuracy and ability to work in our favor.

For my client Brianna, mindfulness was initially a foreign concept. As a highly sought-after thought leader in public health, her mind was always racing, planning her next move and thinking through every possible outcome. During a particularly intense week of research in preparation for a national health disparities intervention rollout she was leading, Brianna shared with me in our coaching session that she loved her work. Still, the intensity and pace sometimes gave her the sensation of drowning. Even as a respected authority in her field, she was stressed and second-guessing herself.

So, I guided her on the three core actions of the activating mindfulness cheat code to build her intuitive capabilities and help her regain trust in herself. I directed her to be intentional, to breathe, and to move. First, I suggested she set an intention around how she wanted to show up as a leader in this important initiative. Though it was heavy work, she intended to bring hope, encouragement, and actionable solutions.

Next, I suggested she take a few minutes each day to sit and breathe. I instructed her to be intentional about the moment, to relax her shoulders, make sure her feet were flat on the floor, and release the clench in her jaw. She said, "Wow, I didn't even realize I was clenching my jaw until you mentioned it."

Her final task was to move. Though she worked in the field of health and wellness, long days and even longer nights in front of her laptop left little time for physical fitness. I told her to start with standing and a two-minute two-step. She chuckled at first, but through my smirk she saw I was dead serious. I shared with her that sitting is the new smoking. This new silent killer lulls us into chronic disease states fueled by sedentary lifestyles. So, any chance she got, her assignment was to stand, and every other hour, she was to break into a two-step for a minimum of two minutes. I explained to her that movement shifts our mood. We could have the same exact schedule from one day to the next. However, the days where movement is incorporated are the days that will feel more productive and more satisfying.

Still skeptical but desperate for relief, Brianna gave it a try. That Monday, she had fifteen minutes before logging on for her next meeting. Instead of poring over her notes, she grabbed her phone and set a timer for seven minutes. For the first five minutes, she sat still in a comfortable position and breathed as instructed, allowing her breath to go deep while she expanded and contracted her belly. Simultaneously, she silently repeated her intention to be a beacon of hope and solutions. She spent the last two minutes doing a fun little two-step, and then when the time was up, she logged on and rocked out in her meeting.

She repeated those same steps during each of the next few days. Those moments, although brief, began to slow the frantic pace in her head while magnifying her confidence. Noticing this, she started seeking out small pockets of time a couple of minutes before a meeting, a few minutes after lunch, and even before she fell asleep at night. For the first time, she could separate herself from the noise and simply *be*. When Brianna reported back to me, the results had her astonished. "Lakila, I was expecting to feel a little less stress, but what's shocked me the most is this feeling of what I can only describe as "mojo"… like if I shoot a shot, I can't miss!" She went on to share that she just knew what to do and knew what to say without a second thought. I told her she described what happens when we give our intuitive capabilities the fuel they need to kick into high gear. Feeding our subconscious through intention-setting, regulating our nervous system with breathing, and boosting our energetic presence with movement is a potent mindfulness-infused cocktail.

With renewed confidence and her intuition clicking on all cylinders, Brianna went on to win a massive seven-figure grant to support her work in healthcare disparities. More than a beacon of hope, her use of the Sho' Nuff Principle and mindfulness made her a force.

Mindfulness isn't about perfection. It's about action, even if that action simply starts wherever you are with the smallest step, make that a jazzy little two-step.

Mindfulness in My Life

Activating mindfulness was clutch in my own life when I found myself in one of the most emotionally taxing moments I could imagine, caring for my terminally ill mother while carrying my first child. It was a season of profound sorrow and profound joy, happening all at once. There were days when it felt like the weight of both of those realities could easily sink my battleship.

During that time, I activated mindfulness as if my life depended on it. And I made no attempt to be some superwoman who could handle it all. I also didn't wake up one day with all the answers or the ability to instantly calm my mind. What I did do was activate mindfulness by setting my intentions, breathing, and moving.

When I was with my mom, I set my intention to be fully with her. And when my mind wandered to my to-do list or the fear of losing her, I used my breath to bring me back to the present moment, whether it was talking, laughing, or sitting quietly by her side. These were moments I would later cherish dearly when she was no longer physically with me. When I was preparing for my son's arrival, I acted with the intention of fondly remembering my pregnancy when it was over and how healthy I wanted my body and son to be. So, I allowed myself to be present for that, too, to feel joy in the magic happening inside my body, and gratitude that both of my mother's and my son's hearts were currently beating in the same dimensional plain at the same time, even if they wouldn't get the opportunity to physically meet. I moved by walking every day for at least twenty to thirty minutes. When my walk turned into a waddle, I continued to do what I could. I took to the pool in the last few weeks of my third trimester, allowing the water to do the heavy lifting for me. But I continued to incorporate daily movement.

Activating mindfulness helped me to intuitively operate with the intention of being a mentally and physically healthy conduit for my mother's and son's energetic connection and to find joy and pride in my role through the transitions of those trying emotional times. We all have moments when life pulls us in opposite directions. That tug-of-war can leave us feeling guilty and scattered. When put into action, mindfulness can be the bridge that allows us to be present for each moment without feeling like we're failing in one space or another.

The Benefits of Mindfulness

Incorporating mindfulness is a potent game changer, and you don't have to devote a ton of time, which you frankly don't have, to put it into practice. Whatever the makeup of your current days or changes to come in your schedule, activating mindfulness is all about building the mindful actions of intention-setting, breathing, and movement into the existing flow of your days.

Mindfulness has some serious benefits, and once you start integrating it into your day, you'll notice a huge difference in how you show up for yourself and others. Here's why it matters:

Reduces stress and anxiety: When you're constantly in "go" mode, your mind and body never get a break. Activating mindfulness helps you create space to be present, regulate your mind and body, and impact the outcome of your experiences. This reduces the stress and anxiety that build up when you're always in motion.

Increases focus and clarity: Have you ever been so overwhelmed that you couldn't think straight? Mindfulness cuts through the noise. By focusing on the present moment, you create mental clarity, which helps you make better decisions and stay focused on what really matters.

Enhances emotional resilience: Life is full of highs and lows, and mindfulness helps you navigate them intuitively. When you're present, you can respond to challenges instead of reacting from a place of panic or frustration. It gives you the emotional resilience to bounce back from setbacks without losing your peace.

Improves well-being: Point blank, mindfulness helps you feel better, mentally, emotionally, and physically. By tuning in to your body's needs, you can better recognize vital lifestyle adjustments like when you need rest, how best to reward yourself, and when to create moments of calm in a busy day.

Practical Ways to Practice Mindfulness

Okay now. Because our time is precious and limited, let's get into the "how." While pausing is a method of activating mindfulness, we can also be active in our mindfulness practice in a way that compliments the natural pace of our lives. There are simple ways to start activating mindfulness today without turning your life upside down. Here, I'll break down the methods we've been discussing for integrating mindfulness into your daily routine:

1. Activate your intention.

Our intentions give both conscious and subconscious direction to our days and, ultimately, our lives. When we intend, we want to begin with the end in mind. The end or outcome can be something we desire to happen in the next hour, the next year, or the next fifty years. The timeframe is not especially relevant. What matters most is focusing on the experience we want, and *not* what we don't want.

For example, it's easy to say, "I don't want anyone to get on my nerves today," or "I want to be married, but I know marriage is hard," or "If I want to have a great career, I've got to sacrifice something I love." Those are all outcomes you may desire, but they are being defined by experiences you *don't* want to have. When we're setting our intention, we have the choice to focus on the experience we actually want. You may want to have a marriage that's easy, a day where every interaction is uplifting, or a career that blossoms in alignment with what you love in life. Having those experiences starts with mindfully setting your intention and being thoughtful about how you call experiences into your existence. Applying the Sho' Nuff Principle is how you make that happen, and its effectiveness is multiplied by your intention. To activate your intention:

1. Write it down. This is called *imprinting*.
2. Visualize it. See yourself doing the thing, accomplishing the goal, and experiencing the bliss that comes with your desired outcome.
3. Add color and emotion. In addition to writing it down and visualizing it, add color and emotion to your vision. You can experience those feelings of accomplishment right now in your subconscious mind and in your body well before they ever actually occur.
4. Take action. Whatever steps you can take right now

in the direction of your intention, take them. Do your part. Unforeseen opportunities reward those who act.

5. Rinse and repeat. Be consistent, and don't let your intentions collect dust.

Remember, before you even get out of bed in the morning, take a moment to set an intention for the day that begins with the end in mind. But not just any ol' ending or any ol' beginning. How do you want to feel at the end of your day? What experience(s) do you want to have that day? Recall that when we set our intention, we focus on what we want, not what we don't want. Instead of "I don't want anybody to tick me off and ruin my mood today," you can set an intention by saying, "I am easily and enjoyably interacting with everyone I encounter today." Using an "I am" statement is a great tool for intention-setting, as it focuses on framing your intention in the affirmative.

2. Activate your breathing.

Your breath is the bomb, and it's one of the most powerful tools you have because you can use it anytime and anywhere. Most of the day, we're breathing on autopilot, and thank goodness for that, because none of us would make it if we had to remember to breathe on our own. Most of our breathing is shallow breaths that do a great job of keeping us alive, but there's so much more our breath can do. When we breathe deeply, we allow stress and anxiety the opportunity to escape our bodies. When feeling overwhelmed, stressed, or scattered, pause and take three deep breaths. Inhale for four counts, hold for four counts and exhale for four counts. Or, if you need to feed yourself some hype energy to engage in a situation requiring your vibrance, you can practice breaths of fire.

There are a ton of breathing techniques out there that serve different purposes. I have a whole team of mindfulness coaches and therapists who teach our clients how to best utilize their breath. The biggest takeaway here is that your breath is your tool, and it's right there at your disposal, so put it to good use.

3. Activate with movement.

As with our breath, we can use movement to slow our racing minds down or to pump our adrenaline up. Movement shifts our mood. No matter what kind of mood you're in beforehand, after a good dose of movement, you've just given yourself a nice little bump of mood enhancer, also known as oxytocin, so you're bound to see an improvement in how you feel. Oh, and your household and colleagues will thank you.

Movement is a multifaceted tool. And it doesn't require hours in the gym or a CrossFit membership, but it's cool if that's how you get down. One of the main reasons we don't move is because we don't feel we have the time. This is where intentional movement saves the day. A study published in the Journal of Happiness Studies found that as little as two minutes of light-intensity physical activity, such as stretching or walking, can improve mood and well-being. So, find a happy medium and do *one* burpee between Zoom meetings...or whatever floats your boat.

The wonderful thing about our amazing bodies is that they were designed to move. Unfortunately, the modern workplace and much of our society are anchored around a sedentary lifestyle that's not exactly movement-oriented. To activate mindfulness, we need to be intentional about incorporating movement into our lives and our days.

Whether walking, dancing, spending an hour at the gym, or just getting up from your desk at regular intervals, make it a point to move with intention. Instead of rushing through the motions, focus on how your body feels. Notice the ground beneath your feet, the stretch in your muscles, or the rhythm of your movements. Movement is how we get our brains to unknot so we can think or give ourselves the energy needed to actively engage in the brilliance of the lives we've built. Movement also allows us to lock in and be present when we need to, improving our ability to focus and concentrate on tasks.

The Main Thing

Here's the main thing about the main thing: Stress and anxiety can be triggered by both the high moments and the challenging moments in our lives. Activating mindfulness is how we most enjoy the highs and better navigate the challenges. Intention-setting, breathing, and movement are all active mindfulness practices that position you to handle everything that comes your way. And you don't have to get it perfect from the start. It's not about meditating for hours a day or being present 100 percent of the time. It's about prioritizing yourself and finding small ways to bring mindfulness into your everyday life so you can feel more grounded, centered, and at peace.

The beauty of mindfulness is that it meets you where you are. You don't have to overhaul your life to reap the benefits. You can start today by being intentional with the moments you already have and learning to slow down, breathe, and incorporate movement, even in the chaos.

Trust me when I tell you that activating mindfulness incites the shift you need to feel more in control of your time, your energy, and your emotions. You'll start to respond to whatever life has in store for you from a place of greater intuitive capability, operating by flow rather than force.

Takeaways:

1. **Mindfulness is a stress antidote.** Mindfulness allows us to be fully present, and our presence incites calm and regulates feelings of calamity.

2. **Give your intuition a boost.** Activating mindfulness is like putting a battery in the back of our intuition, which helps us know what to do and when to do it.

3. **Keep winning all around.** The benefits of mindfulness can show up in every facet of our lives, from the high-impact to the mundane. It's clutch that the tools to activate mindfulness, intention, breath, and movement are easily accessible, and critical that we consistently make use of them.

4. **Engage in practical practice.** You don't have to pack up your life and move to an alpaca farm in order to activate mindfulness. You can incorporate intention-setting, breathing, and movement into the flow of your day and look for opportunities to expand your efforts. (Pro Tip: Activating mindfulness is a great area to apply the Take Two practice.)

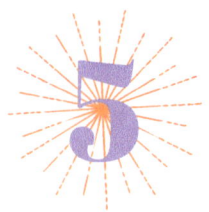

Cheat Code Three: Build Your Support Squad

"Because self-care doesn't mean by yourself."—LJB

An Icy Ivory Tower Becomes a Lighthouse

Isolation can present a juxtaposition of the feeling of safety and extreme loneliness. Asia knew this feeling well. A longtime client of mine and a driven entrepreneur, she built her media company from the ground up, convincing herself along the way that showing vulnerability was a luxury she couldn't afford. By the time we met, burnout had long become a frequent visitor. Over the course of our sessions together, it became clear that Asia was "Squadless." Even though she had a mentor in the media space, she rarely had more than surface-level conversations with her. She never revealed her true challenges for fear of looking weak or incompetent. I asked Asia, "Okay, I get that you don't want to reveal your soft underbelly, but when you have wins, who do you share them with?" She looked at me with a straight face and said, "Well, no one. I accepted a long time ago that I don't want to deal with the backlash of jealousy, and plus, people have their own lives." Asia had insulated herself as a form of protection, but when we build walls to keep others out, we also trap ourselves inside.

I wish Asia's mindset was rare, but it's one I've encountered often when working with high-achieving women. Women have been pitted against each other for as long as women have been in the workforce. We've been taught that we can't or shouldn't ask for help. We've done it all solo dolo for so long that we think that's just the way it is. Asia's mindset reflected all of those things, and it's a recipe for burnout and a lonely life. When we're closed off, we deter and repel. It could be that no one shows up to support or help because your energy reads as if you don't need it. But when we're receptive to goodness, it shows up. When we're intentional about surrounding ourselves with supportive people, they show up.

Asia was intrigued when I introduced her to the Sho' Nuff Principle and the Squad Principle. I pointed out that she's been telling herself all this time that she didn't need anyone and, therefore, had no one in her corner. A slightly embarrassed look washed over her face, and she replied, "I can't afford to have people fail me." I gently countered, "You can tell yourself people will fail you, and they most likely will. Or you can invite in the energy of people you can rely on, who cheer for you, and who are happy to lend their resources and support and watch them conspire in your favor." After some reluctance, Asia eventually embraced the Squad Principle, starting with allowing her team and peers to support her, which led to growth in her already thriving business and, to her surprise, a more fulfilled personal life. It was this shift that turned her business from an icy ivory tower with her trapped inside to a lighthouse for talent and coveted collaborations that allowed her to scale.

In one of our more recent sessions, Asia reflected on the days when she thought pushing through in isolation was a badge of honor. But the Sho' Nuff Principle taught her that the messages she told herself could be rewritten to invite the right people into her life. The Squad Principle showed her that real strength was knowing when to lean on her squad. Now, she didn't just show up for her team and her people; they showed up for her, too, creating a cycle of support and success.

Self-Care Doesn't Mean Doing It Alone

Don't fall for the scam. You were never meant to do it all by yourself, and that includes self-care. I don't care how strong, capable, or independent you are, none of us can thrive without support. The idea that we have to be the strong one all the time, handling every responsibility alone, is a lie high-achieving women have been fed for far too long. It's time to let that go.

A huge part of self-care involves intentionally curating groups of people from your personal and professional life who are down for you like four flat tires. This is where what I call The Squad Principle comes into play. The Squad Principle acknowledges that we draw energy, encouragement, and solutions from the people we surround ourselves with. And it's not about the quantity of people; it's about the quality of the attributes they bring to the table that add value to your life. One person can possess many attributes that contribute to your well-being, or you may find the attributes you need scattered across multiple people. True self-care includes leaning on others, asking for help, and surrounding yourself with the right people in your corner who will support you. This is where your Support Squad is essential. Trust me, you need one.

What Is a Support Squad?

Your Support Squad is made up of the people who have your back. They're the ones who cheer you on when you're winning and pick you up when you fall. They're your confidants, your hype squad, and those who aren't afraid to tell you the hard truths when you need to hear them.

But building a Support Squad isn't just about surrounding yourself with people who will tell you what you want to hear. It's about finding those who will challenge you to be your best self, remind you to rest before you're running on fumes, and celebrate your wins like they're their own.

Some of us, social butterflies, have a contact list full of people who show up for us in different ways and can be relied on. Others of us keep our circles tight and small and may even have only one or two people we'd consider as our Support Squad. I want to reemphasize that your support squad is not about the number of people but the quality of the attributes they bring to your life. Now, it's always a concern for me when I hear people say they don't have anyone they can call on or rely on. Not one person? There's a red flag there, and it's typically associated with the person telling me they can't rely on anyone. We attract the energy we resonate with, and we must intentionally develop our relationships as we evolve in our own life journeys. Maybe as you take inventory of the people in your life, you notice they don't possess any attributes contributing to your growth and wellness. If that's the case, it's time to start redirecting how you spend your time and where you spend your energy. Your people and/or person are out there; it takes intentional effort on both sides to strengthen those connections.

Your Support Squad is an essential part of self-care. They're there to pour into you with ideas, resources, compliments, and encouragement. They're the link in the expansion of your network, as their network ideally becomes your network. They raise your net worth, as net worth often mirrors within a range of the people we spend the most time with.

The Power of Asking for Help

If you're anything like I once was, asking for help might feel like a struggle. We've been conditioned to believe that needing help is a sign of weakness or failure. But let me tell you right now: it's the opposite. Asking for help is one of the strongest, smartest things you can do. It's one of the things that makes intentionally building your Support Squad a key component of self-care and my third cheat code.

When I was juggling the role of caregiver for my mother while preparing for the arrival of my first child, I knew I couldn't do it all. I had to lean on my Support Squad in ways I wasn't used to. I reached out to family, friends, and members of my own Support Squad to help with things that, under different circumstances, I might have tried to handle on my own.

Asking for help can be awkward and hard at first. You feel you should be able to do it all. You may fear being let down or things not being handled to your standards. Yes, that's a risk, especially if your Support Squad is underdeveloped. However, once the intention is to curate a Support Squad, reliability and capability become significantly less of a concern. What I found by allowing others to help me was that, yes, there were things I could have done myself, but certain members of my Support Squad were so much better at those things that the outcome was way better than if I'd handled them on my own. Plus, I was able to show up more fully for both my mother and my baby. I had more energy, more clarity, and more peace. My Support Squad made it possible for me to care for the people I loved while still taking care of myself.

Who Should Be in Your Support Squad?

Now that you know the importance of having a Support Squad, consider who should be in it. Not everyone deserves a seat at your table, so you've got to be intentional about who you allow into your inner circle. Here's what I look for:

Powerfully positive people: These are people who look for the light in any situation, and while they recognize challenges, they don't succumb to them. They see you doing hard things, new things, things you've done a million times, and they reaffirm that you've got what it takes to succeed.

People who brighten your light: These are the ones who bring out the best parts of you. They're the ones who celebrate your wins and help you view "losses" as lessons. They're the people who remind you of your worth when you forget it yourself.

People who keep it real: You need people in your corner who will tell you the truth, even when it's hard to hear. These are the ones who call you out when you're slipping, who hold you accountable to your goals, and who won't let you settle for less than what you deserve. And they do it with care.

People who bring peace: Life is already chaotic enough. You don't need drama or negativity from the people around you. Your Support Squad should be a source of peace and calm, a refuge you can turn to whether the sea of life is still or making waves.

People who share your values: Your squad should align with your core values and vision for your life. These people support your goals, respect your boundaries, and encourage you to live authentically.

Kamille's Race: Running with Vision

The number one member of my Support Squad, next to my husband and son, is my sister and company co-founder, Dr. Kamille Richardson. Kamille is a unique company founder. She was born blind and has never had sight her entire life. Kamille and I are only ten and a half months apart in age and have always been extremely close. So, for my entire life, I've had a front-row seat in knowing that while Kamille wasn't born with the gift of sight, she's always lived with vision. Our mother was the original visionary who could always see more in Kamille and me than we could see in ourselves. Like the time when Kamille and I were in high school and our Mom got the bright idea that Kamille should join our high school track team. You should know that my sister is many things, but at that time, an athlete was not one of them. She was the chorus girl in our household; I was the athlete. But our mom insisted that she try. Which meant she was doing it.

So, I was all pumped when Kamille came home from her first track practice. I asked her how it was. She said, "*HARD!*" and grumpily stormed off to bed. But in true Kamille fashion, she stuck with it and gave it her best.

Eventually, the day for her first meet rolled around. This meet was happening at another school where no one really knew Kamille. She was running a race called the 400, one lap around the track, the longest sprint. To this day, when she describes that time, she'll tell you, "I get on the line…sweating bullets and a whole ball of nerves. My heart is pounding out of my chest so loud I'm sure everyone can hear it. Then the gun goes off, and I start running faster than I've ever run before. I'm sure my lungs are collapsing with every step I take, but I keep on running. Early in the race, I can hear the footsteps of other runners around me, but then, *I didn't hear anybody.*"

Now, I was watching from the stands. She couldn't hear anyone because the other girls had taken off. They were halfway around the track, and Kamille was in dead last place.

People in the crowd began to murmur, "Why is that girl so far behind, and why is she running with somebody?" They soon learned she was blind, and Kamille was running with a guide to prevent her from veering into other lanes. That revelation changed everything. As Kamille reached the final straightaway, a hush fell over the crowd. Then, the most magnificent thing happened as she pushed into that final stretch: The entire crowd, competitors included, erupted in thunderous applause.

Every time Kamille felt like she couldn't go on, she'd hear their voices and encouragement, which gave her the strength to keep pushing. She finished that race strong, not just because of her determination, but because she had her squad lifting her up. You see, Kamille couldn't see how close she was to the finish line, and as a new runner, 400 meters felt like 400 miles. When she was ready to give up, the crowd's cheers let her know the finish line was within reach, so she kept on running. She allowed the crowd to guide her into her own personal victory, sight unseen.

Kamille's race was a testament to the Sho' Nuff Principle in action via The Squad Principle. In preparation for her race, she spent just as much time psyching herself up, telling herself she could do it, as she did training on the track. During the actual meet, when Kamille reached the point that she didn't feel like she had the juice to make it to the finish, The Squad Principle kicked in, as everyone in the stands became her squad that day, giving her a boost of encouragement in the last leg of her race. Our mother was the leader of our Support Squad. She showed Kamille and me that we could do hard things, even in spaces where we had no prior experience. It led me to the executive levels of corporate leadership and later to boldly retire from corporate at just thirty-seven years old to successfully pursue entrepreneurship when no one in my immediate family had taken a similar path.

So just as Kamille needed support on that track, so do we all in our daily races. You need someone like my Mom, who sees and encourages you to step out of your comfort zone. You need someone like Kamille's running guide to keep you from veering into other lanes when distractions arise. You need someone like the crowd who gets wrapped up in the fact that you're making a valiant effort and meets your effort with exuberant applause and encouragement. You also need someone who sees when you're nearing exhaustion and who tells you it's okay to rest, take a break, and pick back up from a place of rejuvenation.

Without delay, I encourage you to build, curate, and nurture your own Support Squad, people who will propel you to thrive beyond your limits. Life's races are won with individual grit and collective encouragement.

How to Build Your Support Squad

Building your Support Squad is as much an investment in you as it is in other people. It takes time, intentionality, and sometimes, a little bit of trial and error. But here's how you can start:

> **Identify the gaps:** Take a look at your current support system. Are there areas where you're lacking support? You may need a mentor to guide you professionally or a friend who will check in on your emotional well-being.

Identifying the gaps will help you figure out what kind of support you need.

Cultivate existing relationships: Sometimes, the people you need are already in your life, you just haven't leaned on them yet. Reach out to those friends or colleagues who have been there for you in the past and ask for more consistent support. Be clear about what you need, and be sure to reciprocate.

Be selective: Not everyone belongs in your squad. Be mindful of who you let into your inner circle. Look for people who bring positive energy, who have your best interests at heart, and who are willing to show up for you the way you show up for them.

Communicate your needs: Your squad can't support you if they don't know what you need. Don't assume that people will automatically know how to help you. Be clear, direct, and specific about what kind of support you're looking for, whether it's someone to listen, someone to offer advice, or someone to help you tackle a big project.

Extend appropriate grace: We all live lives of competing responsibilities and priorities. While you should absolutely curate a reliable Support Squad, understand that everyone is navigating their own hurdles in life and may not always be able to show up in the capacity that you desire at the moment. I encourage you to avoid "throwing the baby out with the bath water." This means taking a moment to assess whether that person has been consistent in how they've shown up in the past and using discernment in deciding to extend appropriate grace versus choosing to feel abandoned and losing a high-value relationship.

It's Okay to Let People Go

I need to add a little something here: not everyone who's in your life right now is meant to stay. There will be times when you need to reevaluate your relationships and make the difficult decision to let some people go. And guess what? That's okay.

Sometimes, people grow apart. Sometimes, relationships become toxic or one-sided. And as hard as it may be, part of building a strong Support Squad is knowing when to cut ties with people who no longer serve your best interests.

It doesn't mean you're cutting them off with malice. It just means you're making space for the relationships that will truly support and nurture you. If you're cutting off people left and right, it could be a sign of growth or the need to exercise better discernment upfront. Also, leave space to receive and be open to new relationships. It sometimes seems easier to lean into the narrative of "no new friends" while closing yourself off to new connections. I've personally developed deep and meaningful relationships at every stage of my life and am excited by the fact that more beautiful relationships await me as I keep living.

The Main Thing

Here's the main thing about the main thing: You don't have to do it alone. In fact, you were never meant to. Building a Support Squad is one of the most powerful forms of self-care you can practice. Recognizing that you deserve a community of people who uplift you, support you, and remind you of your worth, while intentionally nurturing and building relationships, is an invaluable practice of self-care.

Surrounding yourself with people who have your back, push you to grow, and offer you peace when life gets overwhelming will serve you in every stage and phase of your life and career.

In the next chapter, we'll talk about the power of celebrating yourself, and why it's essential to your success. But for now, please take a moment and think about your Support Squad. Who's in it? Who do you need to bring in? And who do you need to let go of? Your success, your peace, and your well-being are all amplified by a strong Support Squad.

Takeaways:

1. **You don't have to do it alone.** Building a strong support system is essential for your personal and professional success and sanity.

2. **Surround yourself with lighters.** Your support squad should include people who spark your internal light, challenge you to grow, and celebrate your wins.

3. **Vulnerability strengthens connections.** Being open and vulnerable with your support squad creates deeper, more meaningful relationships.

4. **Reciprocity is key.** Support is a two-way street. Give back to your squad and create a community of mutual empowerment.

PART TWO

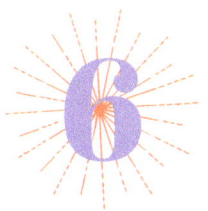

The Celebration Factor

"The secret to enjoying your journey?
Clap while you climb."—LJB

Allow me to welcome you behind the velvet rope and offer you a glass of champagne as we enter what I like to call the VIP section of the Sho' Nuff Principle: The Celebration Factor! The Celebration Factor is the part of The Sho' Nuff Principle where we throw our hands in the air and wave 'em like we just don't care. It's where we pop our collars, toot our own horns, and shimmy our shoulders in acknowledgement of our awesomeness. The first part of this book was all about giving ourselves permission to prioritize self-care. The second part is all about leveraging The Sho' Nuff Principle for our own personal turn-up in self-celebration, self-promotion, and self-advocacy. There ain't no party like a Sho' Nuff party, 'cause a Sho' Nuff party don't stop.

The Celebration Factor is how you become unapologetic about sharing your wins, talents, and accomplishments by doing it in a celebratory fashion, thereby amplifying your results and impact. In other words, we celebrate to elevate and accelerate. You've been out here doing your thing at home, at work, and in life, and it's time to stop being your best-kept secret. This includes self-promotion, but it isn't just about bragging for bragging's sake. It's about owning your value, claiming your space, and promoting yourself in a way that appropriately acknowledges your efforts, elevates your profile, and accelerates your success.

The Celebration Factor ensures that we feel as accomplished as we are. It's also high-key, another form of self-care and burnout prevention. I know and meet way too many high-achieving women who've allowed their achievements to pass without acknowledgment, which is like throwing a blanket over a campfire, smothering the flames. Many believe that if they keep their heads down, their work will speak for itself. But that strategy too often leads to underappreciation, frustration, and burnout. We can totally avoid that by advocating for ourselves and celebrating our journeys as they unfold. Or, as I like to say, by clapping while we climb.

What Is The Celebration Factor?

The Celebration Factor is the battery in the back of our big and small wins. When you get into the practice of acknowledging and rewarding your performance achievements, both personal and professional, in an authentically celebratory fashion, it builds a momentum of winning. Oh, and now you're really enjoying yourself and having fun, too. It puts you in the driver's seat of being your biggest champion, including telling your story, promoting your wins, and ensuring you're leveraging the value you bring to the table and the light you exude in the room.

We, as women, tend to shy away from this. When polling my clients about celebrating themselves and sharing their wins, the most commonly used description was that they were "uncomfortable" with it. And that's no surprise. As a matter of fact, women feel uncomfortable for entirely legit reasons.

On top of the fact that we've been taught that celebrating our success is boastful and that advocating for ourselves is aggressive, there's a whole double standard that women face when it's perceived that we're a little too high on the horse. In our careers, we often lack the support needed to feel comfortable. This dynamic isn't limited to the workplace, it applies at home, too. At home, we're expected to do these incredible things like raising humans and maintaining our households with little to no acknowledgment of the invisible loads they create and that we carry. Society has a whole set of old, raggedy, dated expectations that overemphasize imbalanced humility for women. Women are expected to be the home and office background singers but never the stars. Given all of this, some of us are more comfortable waiting for someone else to recognize our contributions, if those contributions are recognized at all. But waiting for validation only holds us back. In this world, especially in the workplace or as an entrepreneur, advocating for yourself positions you to elevate, and celebrating yourself is the fuel for acceleration.

Self-promotion and self-celebration are skills that, once refined and developed, elevate you as a leader and expert. More meaningfully, they honor your gifts, contributions, and talents. Self-promotion and self-reward are acts of gratitude. What you show gratitude for in your life multiplies, accelerating the pace at which your wins flow and the consistency at which you win.

Why the Celebration Factor Is a Big Deal

Too often, women, especially high-achieving women, shrink in the face of their success. We tend to downplay our wins, deflect praise, or wait for someone else to notice. But in doing so, we undermine our own brilliance, and we unintentionally send out the message that we're not as capable or competent. Every time you caveat your accomplishments or talents, you're not only doing yourself a disservice but also your community, your team, and your family, they all benefit when you show up as the most celebrated version of yourself. And that starts with your own acknowledgment.

Yes, The Celebration Factor includes self-promotion and parties, and it's also about understanding the cumulative and residual impacts of consistent self-recognition. Women who actively promote their achievements and celebrate their wins

- combat impostor syndrome,

- boost their confidence,

- facilitate better networking opportunities and stronger relationships, and

- inspire others, creating a ripple effect of empowerment.

My personal favorite factor when it comes to accelerating our careers is that we achieve greater compensation. That's right, compensation. Moola. Coins. Or, as I like to say, we make "Mo' money, mo' money, mo' money!" Celebrating your strengths and boldly showcasing what you and your company bring to the table isn't just about feeling good, it directly impacts the bottom line.

For example, when I leaned into celebrating the strengths of my company, I stopped downplaying our wins and instead started highlighting them in client pitches, on social media, and during industry events. I positioned our expertise and track record of success front and center. One particular moment stands out: I openly shared how our innovative strategies for stress management helped a Fortune 500 company reduce employee burnout and boost productivity by 25 percent. Even more telling than the numbers was that that same company renewed our contract beyond our original agreement, which gave me a reason to "brag" about gaining their confidence and repeat patronage. That one case study, along with celebrating my team's role in making it happen, resulted in a six-figure contract with a global corporation seeking similar results.

By unapologetically owning and celebrating our strengths, we secured that contract and opened doors to partnerships and speaking engagements that added even more value to our brand. Celebrating what you bring to the table doesn't just boost your confidence, it reinforces your worth to others. It leads to the kind of compensation that reflects your value.

Ladies, on all fronts, the pros of engaging in celebratory self-promotion far outweigh the cons. We just have to give ourselves permission to get the party started.

Beyond that, celebrating your performance is not just for you, it's also for everyone who looks to you as an example of what's possible. By stepping up and celebrating your successes, you can model what it looks like to be proud and powerful without apology.

The Celebration Factor and The Permission to Power Pyramid

The Celebration Factor goes far beyond talking yourself up. Instead, it's sharing and rewarding your success in a way that demonstrates active gratitude for yourself. In this way, you also inspire and empower others. When you advocate for yourself, you're creating space for other women to do the same. You're showing your team, your community, and the world that it's okay to celebrate success.

As with self-care, the Permission to Power Pyramid also applies to self-celebration. The more we celebrate, the more we lighten our invisible loads. In giving ourselves permission to celebrate our accomplishments and share them more widely, we start to alleviate that discomfort that we feel, which allows us to be more consistent at the second level of the pyramid, which is the practice of celebratory self-promotion and self-reward. And like most things, the more we do it, the more comfortable we become. The more our comfort level increases, the more we start to see the benefits, which gives us peace of mind. Not only do self-promotion and self-celebration work in our favor, but participating in both is of material benefit to the larger organizations we support, as well as our families and communities. You're more productive; you're inspiring to the people around you, especially the women around you, to engage and celebrate in self-promotion. And that's where our Power lies, at the top of the pyramid. Our power is in the realization and actualization of our own internal power to enhance our sphere of impact and declare our own victories.

"Frightening" is how my client Tamara described the thought of self-promotion when I suggested she post and share more about her latest successful transit system upgrade. Tamara was a Senior VP over transit for a heavily populated county known for its transit failures. She'd taken the role as a stretch assignment. She flourished in the face of budget challenges and people resource shortages, yet always eschewed praise for her part in leading a very public turnaround effort. After much prodding on my end, she eventually began posting on her LinkedIn about her role in the process, low-key giving herself a prop or two aimed at celebrating how her work solved a longstanding issue in the community that led to more dignified and efficient travel experiences for the county's patrons. The unexpected benefit was that other county officials from across the country began to reach out to her to seek her expertise. So much so that she realized, at my nudging, that the opportunity existed for a consulting business where she could contract and charge much more than her current salary; she'd positioned herself as an expert, and it didn't require overexaggeration. Acknowledging her wins in an authentic way led to profitably aligned opportunities.

Whether it's on social media, in a team meeting, or during a conversation with a mentor, find opportunities to share what you've accomplished. And when you do, make sure you frame it in a way that highlights the impact of your work, not just what you did, but why it mattered.

Overcoming the Fear of Self-Promotion

Now, let's address the elephant in the room: fear. Fear of being judged. Fear of being seen as arrogant. Fear of standing out too much. These fears are real, and they're valid. But they don't have to control you.

The fear of self-promotion is often rooted in the belief that success should speak for itself. But in reality, it doesn't. Being seen, heard, and recognized are the byproducts of using your voice and actions to acknowledge and celebrate yourself. When you're willing to say, "I did this, and I'm proud of it," you unlock a powerful cycle of growth and positivity.

The more you celebrate yourself, the more there is to be proud of. Success becomes a magnet, drawing in opportunities and activities you genuinely enjoy, and you start to approach your daily life with accomplished energy. This energy fuels your ability to excel in almost anything as you consistently build confidence and momentum. Not to mention, celebrating yourself naturally attracts talent, resources, and support, whether it's through building a formal team or fostering informal networks of champions who want to see you thrive.

The callout here is simple: self-celebration doesn't have to be "cringy." Nor should it be. The more you practice celebrating yourself, the easier and more natural it becomes. And as it becomes second nature, you'll find that your confidence, success, and satisfaction grow exponentially.

The Celebration Factor in Action

You may not know this, but your brain loves a good party. Our brains actually have a built-in system of reward in the form of a complex neural network responsible for reinforcing behaviors, including seeking pleasure and satisfaction. So, achieving small goals strengthens the neural pathways associated with that particular task or skill. Over time, repeated small wins can lead to the development of new neural connections. Through the regular release of dopamine, we can create a positive feedback loop that helps alleviate stress and anxiety and neutralizes fear. That helps us tackle bigger challenges and makes winning our nature (small wins count and lead to bigger wins). And before you get all pre-exhausted at the thought of having to "plan a party" to turn your brain's reward system on, please keep in mind that celebration doesn't have to be elaborate, just intentional and sincere. From a very practical standpoint, life's a hell of a lot more fun when you're celebrating.

Once Tamara began to see how self-acknowledgment and promotion were impacting her career and life, I had her take it a step further and start to integrate intentional celebrations by pausing after each win to reflect on how her contributions and efforts directly led to the win and to connect it to her level of impact. This practice deepened her appreciation for her work and helped her see that self-celebration and acknowledgment served her larger purpose.

When you share your wins with intention, it's more than just an acknowledgment of success; it's a declaration of the value of your contributions, a bridge to collaboration, and an invitation for others to step into their own power.

The Main Thing

Here's the main thing about the main thing: Celebrating yourself, rewarding yourself, and promoting yourself help you "skip the line" when done with intention. When we share our successes thoughtfully and deliberately, advocate for ourselves, and celebrate our wins, we open the door to a multitude of benefits.

Celebrating yourself builds confidence, allowing you to approach challenges with boldness and clarity. It attracts like-minded individuals who want to collaborate, creating stronger networks and partnerships. It also sets the tone for others to respect and recognize your value, leading to promotions, profitable contracts, or new opportunities that align with your goals. On top of that, celebrating yourself amplifies your ability to inspire and empower others, cultivating a ripple effect of positivity and growth.

When you apply The Celebration Factor, you set yourself up to use your success as a springboard for even greater achievements. By incorporating the four final cheat codes, Brag More, Pre-Plan Your Parade, Expect the Best, and Rest Your Bones, you're not just skipping the line; you're building a sustainable path to long-term success and fulfillment. These codes ensure that your celebration isn't just a moment but a *movement*, propelling you forward in every aspect of your life.

Takeaways:

1. **Celebrating yourself fuels your growth.** When you celebrate, you enhance your confidence, neutralize self-doubt, and create energy to tackle bigger goals with boldness and clarity.

2. **Self-promotion is a skill, not a taboo.** By sharing your accomplishments, you position yourself for new opportunities, stronger relationships, and greater recognition in both personal and professional spaces.

3. **Celebration is self-care.** Taking intentional moments to reflect on and reward your achievements keeps you feeling fulfilled, energized, acknowledged, and motivated.

4. **Overcome fear through practice.** The more you advocate for yourself, the more natural and empowering it becomes, making you a stronger leader and role model.

5. **Celebration attracts resources and opportunities.** By showcasing your strengths, you not only acknowledge your value but also attract talent, resources, and partnerships that align with your goals, accelerating your journey toward even greater achievements.

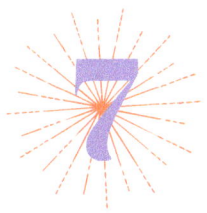

Cheat Code Four: Brag More

"Bragging is not a bad b-word, nor does it make you a bad b-word."—LJB

The Celebration Factor is activated by practicing the fourth cheat code of bragging more. One of the origins of the name for The Sho' Nuff Principle comes from here: Whenever I would give myself props (aka brag) on something I'd done well, like delivering a keynote for instance, someone would add on with a compliment; I'd follow their compliment with an enthusiastic "Sho' Nuff" or "Sho' you right!" or "Sho'll am!" versus "I know, but I've been doing this a long time. I made a lot of mistakes to get this good." Or "I know, but I've got to get better at closing after my talks." Or "Thank you. I'm trying." The fact is I'm never "trying." I'm doing. When there's an opportunity to do what we do better, it may make sense to strive to improve, but we underestimate how much we improve by simply acknowledging with enthusiastic pride what we've already done without caveat, slight, or self-humbling remark.

Self-Promotion: Own Your Wins!

Women should brag more. A lot more. We've been sold a dream that if we work hard enough, the reward, promotion, acknowledgment, and so on will eventually come. It may. But it also may not. As a high-achieving woman, you've earned every accomplishment, every success, and every milestone. And when you personally acknowledge your achievements, you amplify the rewards and recognition that rightfully come along with those achievements.

Bragging or self-promotion isn't just about getting that raise or promotion at work (though you absolutely deserve that, too). It's about recognizing your own value and owning your worth unapologetically. It's about being proud of who you are and what you bring to the table, and making sure the energy you project to everyone around you reflects exactly that. Self-promotion conveys confidence, and that confidence translates to others in affirming your capability. Trust me, as a woman, you can stand to brag more.

Owning your achievements and speaking up about them authentically lands you in a place of genuine and trusted authority. It becomes clear that you know your sh—stuff. This leads to deserved recognition, promotion, and being paid for the value you bring. More than that, you demonstrate self-appreciation and receive more demonstrated outward appreciation. I don't just mean empty language about how much you're appreciated; I mean the people around you becoming more consistent at demonstrating that they appreciate you with their actions and respect. But first, you've got to get comfortable talking about yourself in a positive, non-deprecating manner and stop giving an imbalanced amount of attention to your development areas and weaknesses. To effectively execute the self-promotion cheat code, focus on the areas where you're regularly operating in your zone of genius. Focusing on your strengths and what you do well and enjoy is the low-hanging fruit where you can experience the most exponential growth, especially when you drop the saddlebags of self-deprecation.

Why Bragging Is Essential

Before you start thinking, "But Lakila, I don't want to come off as arrogant," let me be clear that I am not advocating for being obnoxious. Bragging, in the context of being a cheat code, isn't about arrogance, it's the act of warranted self-advocacy and self-promotion. It's taking up space, owning your accomplishments, and letting people know that you're out here doing the damn thing. How will people know if you don't talk about your wins? How can you alleviate the blind spots so your stakeholders see the value you're bringing to the team? How are potential clients supposed to know you're the best at what you do? How will your kids truly grasp how awesome of a mom they have? You might be thinking, "Well, Lakila, I show them with my actions." But here's the thing, actions alone often aren't enough. Think about all the supermoms you know, yourself included, perhaps, and how many feel underappreciated and burned out despite doing it all. The recognition just isn't there, and it ties right back to the martyrdom of womanhood we discussed in the introduction.

That's why I always say that as much as silent movies were a thing of the past, blockbusters thrive on dialogue. In other words, your actions hit differently when your words amplify them. Talking it like you're walking it, that's The Celebration Factor in full effect. When you name and claim your wins, you affirm your value and show others how to appreciate and celebrate you properly.

Bragging in this context is proactively expressing pride in your work and efforts, and confidence in your performance. And you know what? Men brag all the time, even when it's unwarranted.

They're out here promoting themselves, putting their wins on display, and getting the recognition (and money) that comes with it. Now, I'm not telling you to act like a lady and think like a man. I'm telling you to leverage The Sho' Nuff Principle to tap into your divine feminine energy, using your innate power of persuasion to convey your authentic talents, gifts, and accomplishments. Your authenticity is the key to owning your relationships and inter-actions in a proprietary way. Remember that you're not making things up; you're talking about things you've actually done or can do. The goals you've met or blown out of the water. Challenges you've taken on and applied valuable lessons from in both your professional and personal life. Just as you teach others how to treat you based on how you treat yourself, so too do you teach others how to think about you based on how you demonstrate that you think about yourself.

Let's recall from a previous chapter my former colleague, Tina. During our morning leadership meetings, Tina skipped over the disposable white cups and coffee and drank tea from a proper tea cup "because it was just one of [her] little delights" and a part of her personal self-care routine. I shared that Tina's teacup was an example of how Tina treated herself with care, and therefore, so did everyone else, whether they were more senior, peers, or direct reports.

The story doesn't stop there. I was on a ride-along with Tina one day, and in talking, I got to know her beyond the teacup. Tina's teacup reminded her of her dignified grandmother, a woman of influence in her Guyanese community. Tina's grandma "got stuff done." Also, Tina retired as an officer in the Navy before joining our healthcare firm; she understood the power of percep-tion, how it impacted the troops' willingness to rally behind her, and how it led to her military superiors granting her support and resources. Now, in the corporate environment, Tina's teacup was a way of visually differentiating the caliber of her performance from that of her peers, beyond simply putting in the work.

Sometimes, we think all we have to do is put in the work. Surely people are going to know how great we are based on that alone, and that we should be promoted, that we're more than qualified for an opportunity, or that we're the heartbeat of our households.

I've got news. They're not going to know, not solely based on your performance.

Tina's regions exceeded key performance metrics, but even when the occasional operational hiccup happened, Tina was able to garner the breathing room she needed to sort it out without backlash because she consistently reinforced the narrative of being an accomplished leader who delivered results. She reinforced that narrative to her mentors, direct reports, and sponsors, who all, in turn, championed that same message. And Tina never missed an opportunity to celebrate her accolades and promotions in a way that excited others to celebrate her as well.

Why Do We Hold Back?

In all fairness, bragging doesn't come naturally to most of us, especially as women. I can't tell you how many brilliant women I've met who are doing incredible things but are afraid or too uncomfortable to speak up about it. They worry that people will think they're full of themselves or that they'll be judged for talking about their accomplishments. So, they downplay their achievements, deflect praise, and avoid the spotlight. But here's the deal: Haters are gonna hate, don't let the possibility of hateration make you play small. Holding back your greatness doesn't serve your higher purpose. In fact, it does the opposite. When you downplay your success, you're not just dimming your own light; you're robbing others of the opportunity to learn from you, be inspired by you, or even collaborate with you. It's time to stop worrying about what other people will think and start owning your wins. Plus, the people who're more willing to negatively judge or downplay your accomplishments are not the people who belong in your Squad.

The Power of Bragging

Bragging, when done right, is powerful. It positions you as a leader, an expert, and someone who knows your worth. It opens doors, creates opportunities, and builds your reputation. When you brag more, people take notice. They start to see you as someone who knows her value and isn't afraid to claim it.

How to Brag (Without Feeling Weird About It)

Now, I know bragging can feel uncomfortable at first, especially if you're not used to it. But keep in mind that you're deserving of props. You don't have to embellish. And, like anything, it gets easier with practice. Here are a few tips to help you brag more unapologetically:

1. Keep a "brag bag."

One of the best ways to start bragging more is to create a "Brag Bag." This is a list of all your wins, accomplishments, and milestones, big or small. It could be a major project you led, a client testimonial highlighting your brilliance, or even a small win like finally nailing a difficult task. Some of the items in my Brag Bag at the time of writing this book included closing on a coveted recurring revenue agreement with a major corporate client, establishing my family's trust, and potty training my son. Oh, and finishing this book!

Keep your brag bag somewhere handy, like in your notes app, and add everything from major project milestones to positive feedback emails. I also recommend putting the highlights somewhere where you can see them. Over time, it becomes your go-to confidence boost before big meetings, tough family conversations, or any random anxiety-inducing moment. Reviewing your list reminds you of the impact you make every day and prepares you to share your successes with conviction.

2. Start small.

If the idea of bragging still makes you feel uneasy, start small. The next time someone compliments you, don't deflect. Accept it, own it, and add a little bit of bragging in response. For example, if someone says, "Great job on that project," instead of saying, "Oh, it was nothing," say, "Thank you! I impressed myself, and I'm really proud of how it turned out."

I start many of my clients with the first step in this direction: accepting compliments without deflection. I encourage them to initiate a process of pride in themselves when sharing an accomplishment. I also guide them to follow the compliments they receive with words of affirmation such as "That's my gift" or "Thank you. That's how I roll." While seemingly small, these changes are significant, signaling a shift toward owning their achievements.

3. Use facts and results.

One of the easiest ways to brag without feeling weird about it is to use facts and results. This takes the focus off of you as a person and puts it on the measurable outcomes of your work. Instead of saying, "I'm great at managing teams," you could say, "The team I managed increased productivity by 30 percent last quarter." For personal accomplishments, the same applies. A results-based brag could be something like, "After four months of focus on clean eating and daily movement, I'm down twenty pounds and feeling like myself again!"

When we take this approach, we pique curiosity and spark genuine interest, especially in results-driven professional environments where outcomes matter or in situations where details and results provide the much-needed context that highlights how significant an achievement really is.

4. Share the story, not just the win.

Another great way to brag without feeling like you're being too boastful is to share the story behind the win. People love a good story, and sharing the journey, challenges, and lessons you learned along the way makes your achievement even more impressive.

So open up and share the behind-the-scenes story of a major project during that team meeting. Talk to your friends and family about the initial hurdles you've encountered along the way to the creative solutions you implemented and how they led to exceeding expectations for your household. Demonstrate a new level of respect for your own leadership and resilience and allow that energy to resonate with others so they can adopt it, as well.

Bragging Isn't Just for You, It's for Them, Too

I want you to remember something important: bragging isn't just for you. Yes, it's about owning your success and getting the recognition you deserve, but it's also about inspiring others and helping others understand the value that you bring to the table. When discussing your wins, you're giving other women permission to do the same. You're showing them that it's okay to take up space, to claim their value, and to celebrate their greatness. You're also making collaborations, promotions, and aligned opportunities easier because people can trust that you know how to get things done. Confidence in your own abilities often speaks louder than the actions themselves.

Bragging creates a ripple effect. When you show up fully in your power, it encourages other women to do the same. So don't think of bragging as something selfish, think of it as something necessary. You're not just advocating for yourself but setting an example for every woman watching you. You're not just popping your collar; you're reassuring others of your capability and reliability... as you pop your collar. (wink)

Deciding to speak openly about our success can inspire the organizations and households we lead to adopt the same approach. I've seen companies where once-quiet meetings turned into sessions filled with shared wins and strategies. The culture of those companies shifted to one where celebrating success was the norm, and everyone felt encouraged to take ownership of their achievements. Even more fulfilling is when I see my clients follow my guidance to bring the bragging cheat code home to apply it to their home life. In my own household, we have what we call "Mad Props Fridays," where my husband, son, and I give ourselves and each other kudos on the things we're proud of over the week. Not only is it a fun part of our week and a way we connect more deeply with each other, but it's also how we continue to support and encourage each other, building on the momentum of winning in our house.

Let's Start Bragging

Here's your challenge for this week: I want you to start bragging more. It could be something small, sharing a recent win with your boss or posting about a milestone on social media. Or it could be something bigger, like making the case for a promotion or a raise because you know you've earned it. Consider something personal like following through on a commitment to your creative side, nurturing a budding relationship, or learning guitar. Whatever it is, I want you to own it unapologetically.

There's nothing wrong with celebrating your success. You've worked hard for it, and you deserve to be recognized for everything you've accomplished. For women, bragging more is a transformative act of empowerment that boosts confidence, inspires others, and opens doors we may never have thought possible.

The Main Thing

Here's the main thing about the main thing: It ain't bragging if you can do it. It's facts. Okay, it's still bragging, but bragging is not a bad b-word when it's not arrogant or recklessly boastful. Owning your achievements, advocating for yourself, and taking up the space you deserve in a way that's genuine and authentic to you and your style creates opportunities, deepens connections, and builds your reputation as a leader.

In the next chapter, we'll talk about expecting the best and how your mindset shapes your reality. But for now, I want you to focus on bragging more. Take up space. Own your brilliance. And lead your next conversation with how amazing you are!

Takeaways:

1. **Bragging is owning your worth.** When you celebrate your achievements unapologetically, you affirm your value and show others that you understand the incredible contributions you bring to the table.

2. **Action and words work together.** Pairing your actions with intentional self-promotion amplifies your accomplishments and ensures they're seen, heard, and acknowledged.

3. **Confidence is contagious.** This boosts your credibility and attracts opportunities, partnerships, and respect.

4. **Bragging creates a ripple effect.** Your confidence sets a powerful example, encouraging a culture of celebration and empowerment at work, at home, and within your community.

5. **Bragging opens doors.** People can't champion you if they don't know what you've achieved.

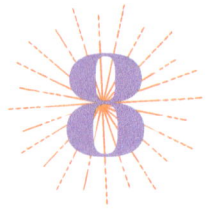

Cheat Code Five: Expect the Best

"You choose 100 percent of your expectations."—LJB

Mindset Shift: What You Expect Is What You'll Experience

One thing about me is that there can be absolutely zero logical or visible reason why a situation should work in my favor, and I'll still expect it to work out in my favor. This practice has never failed me, not once. We've talked about owning your wins, bragging more, and building that Support Squad. Now, let's get into another cheat code of The Sho' Nuff Principle that can truly shift the way you experience your life: expecting the best.

I know. It almost sounds too simple, right? Well, that's because it really is that simple, what you expect out of life hugely impacts how you experience outcomes in your life. I'm talking about shifting your mindset to active optimism. Active optimism is choosing an optimistic perspective powered by the actions of an optimist. When you expect greatness and believe that good things will come your way, you start making moves that align with those expectations. On the flip side, if you're always expecting the worst, that negative energy seeps into everything you do and shifts the mind in the worst direction.

Have you ever been around someone who approaches everything with hesitation, preparing for criticism and failure before even beginning? This mindset makes them hesitant to take risks but also diminishes their confidence. Subconsciously, they've prepared themselves for failure, and while it may not keep them from making progress, they certainly put a hard limit on what they can accomplish and often miss seizing opportunities that are well within reach.

Say it with me: The best outcome in any situation in which I find myself *is* an option. Period. Whether in your career, relationships, or personal life, you are worthy of receiving the good things you've worked so hard for. But for it to feel like you deserve it, you have to act like you believe it first.

Why Expecting the Best Matters

Think about it: If you walk into a room with your head held high, fully expecting to crush that presentation, negotiate that deal, or land that promotion, you're already halfway there. Your confidence shows. Your energy is magnetic. People are drawn to you because you carry yourself like someone who knows she deserves to win.

I operate with what some may consider a delusional belief in my ability to win at everything. True high achievers have to operate in some realm of delusion to navigate all the hurdles that come along with exceptional levels of success in any area. Every chip may literally be stacked against me: limited access to capital, no family or friend support, very little experience in an arena, and yet, the ability to thrive and overcome the odds still exists by simply anchoring my mindset to expect the best outcome that works out in my favor, and then taking action with that energy.

I'm sure you've heard the expression, "Whether you believe you can or you can't, you're right." Well, the same concept applies to your expectations. In any situation, you can choose to rehearse everything that could go wrong mentally or switch your mindset to expect victory instead of fearing failure. That confidence impacts how you feel, how you present yourself, and the level of capability you exude.

But what happens when you expect the worst? You shrink. You second-guess yourself. You play small, and that energy is just as contagious. When you don't believe in yourself or what you're capable of, it shows. And not only do other people pick up on it, but you start to make decisions from a place of fear instead of poise.

Mindset Is Everything

Your thoughts, your beliefs, and your expectations create the world you live in. You may not have direct control over every circumstance, but you always have 100 percent control over your expectations.

When you expect the best, your brain starts to look for ways to make that happen. You start noticing opportunities that align with your goals. You take bigger, more calculated risks because you're not paralyzed by the fear of failure. You start showing up as the woman who knows she deserves to win, and the universe responds accordingly. I'll take this a step further and say expect things to work out in your favor and even *better* than you expect. Sometimes, our expectations are limited by what we know to be possible, even when oriented on success. But when we build in the option for things to work out better than we expect, we create the space for unforeseen results that we couldn't possibly have fathomed, results that may even have been outside the access of our consciousness.

For example, when I had my son, I decided to focus my attention on healing and rest versus getting back on the grind in my company. I gave myself permission to take the time I needed to heal myself after an emotionally tumultuous pregnancy, to learn to be a mom and to connect with my son. Financially, this was not the logical decision. But intuitively, I knew I could trust my first mind and instinct to rest. When I did decide to return, I set my expectation that everything would work out in my favor and be better than I expected. Were there moments where I was unsure? Certainly. I'm human and no different from any woman reading this book. But I applied the Permission to Power Pyramid and extended myself a ton of grace through positive self-talk. I activated mindfulness like my life depended on it, because it did, and I leaned heavily into my support squad. I also regularly celebrated my decision to choose myself and shared the milestones of my improvements as my mental, emotional, and physical capacity came back into alignment. I treated myself like a solar panel. Those are some of the actions I took to support my expectations.

One night toward the end of this period, just before I went to sleep, I was having a conversation on the phone with my sister, Kamille, cackling per usual, when she mentioned a huge conference she'd been invited to attend and speak at the following month. Something in me awakened, and I said, "I'll fly into town and go with you." Up until that point, I'd been way off the scene. I didn't even own a business casual outfit that currently fit my new beautiful postpartum size. But I felt compelled to go. Well, we did attend, and not only did Kamille knock it out of the park onstage, but I also casually made connections on behalf of our business that led to what was, at the time, our largest commercial contract. That contract became the springboard for multiple larger contracts and speaking engagements to follow that took our fledgling business into the seven-figure realm. None of this was planned. None of it was forced. And despite stepping back into the world of business, I continued to prioritize self-care and self-celebration, so it all happened in flow. The opportunities around me rose to meet and align with my expectations of the best or even better, both in business and in my home life.

When your mindset is stuck in survival mode, when you're always preparing for the worst, that's exactly what you'll attract. You'll miss opportunities because you're too busy worrying about what could go wrong. I could have forced myself back into "Business Betty" mode for fear of losing chances to pad my bank account, becoming less relevant in my field, or appearing unproductive and lazy. And I'm sure I'd have experienced some success if I'd forced myself back out there prematurely, but at what cost to my personal fulfillment? When your expectations are fear or lack-centered, you'll settle for less when you can attract more.

Interestingly enough, several of the high-achieving women I've worked with over the years have amassed much of their success and achievements fueled by an energy of fear. Some have been the first in their family to make it out of their hometown. Others grew up without financial resources, so they've fought tooth and nail to stay away from poverty for fear of ever being broke again. There have also been those who legitimately had to fight every step of the way to prove their worthiness to compete in spaces where it's been made clear they weren't welcome. I've personally been fueled at times in my life and in my early career by every single one of those fear-based reasons. I *over*stand. The reasons women tend to govern their expectations are often out of a necessity to protect themselves. I get that, and while the sentiments are valid, I offer this cheat code as an expansion beyond these logical but limiting beliefs. Equipping yourself with expectations of the best and actions that support those expectations is a much stronger and more effective method of ensuring success is realized and satiating to your soul.

Shoot Your Shot: Expecting the Best in Action

My proclivities toward fearlessness and abundance developed at a young age. When I was in the seventh grade, I played basketball for my junior high school, and I assure you, I wasn't exactly the star of the team. I'd get the ball, and I'd be wide open for a shot. But instead of going for it, I'd hesitate. I'd be so focused on the possibility of missing that I wouldn't even take the shot. I did this several games in a row. After every game, when my father got home from work, he'd ask me, "Did you score today?"

"No," I'd reply.

"Did you shoot?" he'd ask.

"No," I'd reply.

But there was one game where everything changed for me.

One day, my father said, "Don't come home from your game today without shooting the ball." Now, my dad is a gentle giant. But he still has the kind of commanding voice that lets you know when something isn't a request. So, in the very next game, the first time the ball landed in my hands, I launched it toward the basket and hit a three-pointer! The only thing more exhilarating was sharing the news with my dad that evening when he got home from work. His reaction was priceless. He picked me up and swung me around in the air. It was a reaction that was way better than I'd ever expected. And I learned an invaluable lesson: "You've gotta shoot to score." It was a simple but powerful revelation. I realized that I had taken myself out of the game by focusing on the possibility of failure. I had counted myself out before I even gave myself a chance.

From that day on, I made a decision to always shoot my shot, whether it was in basketball or in life. Did I make them all? Heck no. I eventually began to make a lot more than I missed, though. I decided to expect the best outcome, and when I did, everything changed. I started taking risks, making bolder moves, and you know what? Not only did those shots begin to go in, but my confidence in life and off the court expanded with the same energy. In short order, I became a better player because I started expecting to win.

The Law of Resonance

You've probably heard of the Law of Attraction, the idea that what you focus on, you attract. But let me introduce you to something even more powerful: The Law of Resonance.

The Law of Resonance in layman's terms says that what you prepare for is prepared for you. So, when you expect the best and prepare for the best, you're resonating at a higher frequency and you can start aligning your energy, actions, and mindset with the outcome you've prepared yourself to experience.

When you resonate with success, abundance, and greatness and prepare yourself accordingly, you attract more successful, abundant, and great experiences into your life. But here's the catch: If you're always preparing for things to go wrong, guess what? You're elevating your risk of drawing more experiences that align with things going wrong. Your thoughts, actions, and decisions will all reflect that fear of failure, and you're more susceptible to getting exactly what you were trying to avoid in some form. Even when you win, the feeling of winning may be missing or watered down.

By training ourselves to expect the best, we can leverage the Law of Resonance to make more money, attract better relationships (intimate, familial, or professional), and live in alignment with our purpose. We can begin to operate at a higher caliber and attract the higher-caliber people, resources, and opportunities that resonate with the level at which we are living.

So, the question is, what are you resonating? Are you preparing for success? Are you making moves like someone who expects to win? Or are you stuck in a cycle of preparing for the worst, always bracing yourself for failure and calamity?

How to Start Expecting the Best

Wherever you are on the spectrum of expectations, shifting your mindset may not happen overnight. And if you've been living in survival mode for years, it can feel like a foreign concept to start expecting the best. Even if you generally expect good things but haven't been super intentional about explicitly directing your expectations, there's plenty of opportunity to make impactful incremental improvements. Here are a few brave micro and macro actions you can take to start mastering the cheat code of expecting the best in every area of your life:

1. Reframe your fears.

Every time you catch yourself expecting the worst, pause and ask yourself, "What's the *best* thing that could happen?" Instead of focusing on what could go wrong, start thinking about how things could go right. This simple shift in perspective changes the energy you bring to every situation. Some fears stem from legitimate concerns. So, in addition to reframing them, take time to reframe them from a lens of what's within your control. Take action to prevent your concerns from occurring, or at least to minimize their impact. This makes you more empowered and proactive rather than paralyzed by fear or uncertainty. By focusing on the positive possibilities and the actions you can take to influence outcomes, you build confidence and create a sense of agency. This mindset allows you to approach challenges with clarity, resilience, and a readiness to seize opportunities, ultimately increasing your chances of success.

2. Visualize success.

Our mind's eye is an often underutilized but powerful tool at our disposal. So, when you set expectations, take a few minutes each day to visualize the outcome that you desire coming to pass. Whether it's becoming a thought leader in your area of expertise, pivoting into a new professional lane, or, like me, finally establishing the family trust you've been putting off for years, visualize yourself enjoyably operating in the space where it has already been done and you've accomplished the thing, whatever the thing happens to be. Picture it in detail, how you'll feel, what you'll say, and how others will respond. And, just as in Cheat Code 2: Activating Mindfulness, don't forget to add color and emotion. The more you engage in deep visualization, the more your mind will hunt to support and confirm your expectations.

Think of it like a mental rehearsal that gives you a sense of déjà vu when those moments actually happen, making them feel natural and earned.

3. Surround yourself with winners.

Energy is contagious. If you're constantly around people who expect the worst, that negativity is going to rub off on you. But when you surround yourself with people who are winning, expecting the best, and getting it, you'll also feel that energy and be able to draw from it. Just be sure to reciprocate, of course. Your Support Squad should be filled with people who lift you up, believe in you, and expect you to win.

4. Prepare for success, not failure.

Script out your success and how you'll respond when things work out in your favor or better than expected. Go ahead and write the acceptance speech. Plan for how you'll reward yourself. Invest in the support you need to operate at the next level, such as investing in a coach. Stop preparing for things to go wrong. Stop waiting for the other shoe to drop. Instead, start preparing for things to go right.

Embrace the Best-Case Scenario

For many of us, expecting the best may sound risky, especially when we've grown accustomed to managing our expectations as a defense mechanism. We tell ourselves that if we expect the worst or just good enough, we won't be disappointed when things don't go our way. Sometimes, we approach big opportunities with a guarded heart, thinking it will soften the blow of disappointment. When you do that, you aren't truly giving yourself the chance to embrace the best possibilities. The problem with that mindset is that it keeps you stuck. It keeps you from dreaming big, taking risks, and going after what you really want. When we let go of that mindset, we feel freer and more energized to go after what we want without reservation.

Here's what I want you to understand: you are worthy of expecting the best. You don't have to settle for mediocrity. You don't have to brace yourself for failure just because it's possible. You can live a life where good things happen to you on purpose or by happenstance, your hard work pays off, and you can show up as your most well-cared-for and well-celebrated self, confident that success is waiting for you on the other side of any action you take.

The Main Thing

Here's the main thing about the main thing: What you expect is often what you experience, regardless of the actual outcome. If you expect good enough, your experiences reflect as much. But when you shift your mindset to expect the best, you open yourself up to a whole new world of possibilities. You start moving differently, thinking differently, and making decisions from a place of confidence instead of fear.

In the next chapter, we will talk about the power of celebration, why it's so important to intentionally celebrate your wins and how that celebration fuels even greater success. I want you to take a moment and ask yourself: What am I expecting? And if the answer isn't "the best," it's time to start the shift toward active optimism.

Takeaways:

1. **Engage in active optimism.** What you expect shapes your reality, so choose to expect the best to attract confidence, clarity, and success.

2. **Own your worthiness.** Believe you're worthy of success and abundance, and let that belief guide your expectations, actions, and decisions.

3. **Shoot your shot.** Take risks with confidence, focusing on potential rewards rather than fears, and seize the opportunity to grow beyond your current capabilities or limitations.

4. **Expand your expectations beyond the logical.** Logic alone can be limiting when it comes to our expectations of ourselves. Equip yourself with expectations of the best to experience results that defy logic but are entirely realizable.

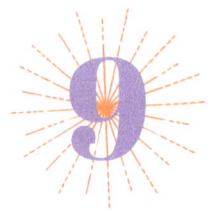

Cheat Code Six:
Pre-Plan Your Parade

"Why would I leave a perfectly good party?"
—Margaret Bowden (my Mother-in-Love)

My Mother-in-Love, Margaret, and her sisters are known for celebrating each other and members of the family, especially for birthdays. So, it was no surprise that she not only played a major role in helping to plan and orchestrate a birthday party for one of her nieces who was turning the Big Three-Oh, but she also was one of the first to the dance floor once the party got underway. When someone suggested the "older crowd" head out and leave the party to the young folks, she turned mid-Wobble, said, "Now, why would I leave a perfectly good party?" and continued on dancing without missing a beat. Her exuberance brought more folks out onto the dance floor, and the party was a hit that we still laugh about to this day!

So, now that we've flexed our bragging muscles and set our expectations on the best, the next step is to fully embrace The Celebration Factor by applying the cheat code of Pre-Planning Your

Parade! Celebrating our accomplishments is vital, our brains thrive on rewards, and our wins grow when we acknowledge them. But knowing isn't enough. To truly harness The Celebration Factor, you need a plan just like my Mother-in-Love, Margaret had. During all of her birthday setup hard work, she was already planning to reward herself with at least a line dance or two. Celebration is crucial for protecting our peace and amplifying our achievements, so we're definitely not leaving it to chance. As the saying goes, "Failing to plan is planning to fail." And then you may miss your chance to Wobble Baby. Wobble Baby. Wobble Baby. Yeah!

So, I want you to pre-plan your parade. I'm talking literally and figuratively, by the way. I mean, who says you can't throw a whole parade for yourself? And by parade, I mean any form of self-celebration that resonates with you and makes you feel rewarded. Your celebrations simply need to be sincere and meaningful to you. They can be as quaint or grand as you choose as long as they're happening. And we improve on making them happen by planning in advance.

Why Pre-Plan?

For some of you, the idea of celebrating yourself may sound appealing. You may even be gung-ho to get started. Or you may have a growing sense of discomfort, even anxiety, at the thought. However you feel, it's perfectly valid. So, to alleviate the potential stress and to set us up for success, we plan for wins that haven't even happened yet. Planning in advance does several things that work in our favor, such as taking the pressure off to decide in the moment how to celebrate yourself when, as a high-achieving woman, chances are your plate is already quite full. When we're busy and in the throes of handling our business, raising families, and trying to drink our body weight in water to stay hydrated, it's easy to resume putting ourselves on the back burner, even if the benefits of doing otherwise are crystal clear. But when you pre-plan how to celebrate your wins, you reduce the chance of skipping celebrating yourself altogether, making the empty promise that you'll return to it or celebrate the next win. Establishing new habits and behavior patterns takes time, which is why this cheat code is so effective. It mitigates an element of our human nature, which is to avoid change, even good change. It also sets us up to be successful at reaping the benefits of The Celebration Factor by backing up the fundamental force of The Sho' Nuff Principle with action. Tell yourself you're going to celebrate yourself, and then put a plan in place to do just that.

One of the most important things pre-planning does is establish in your mind, consciously and subconsciously, that there are more wins to come. Yes, you may have your list. All the things you plan to accomplish over the coming year or years are great. But I want you to supercharge that list by verifying your belief in yourself and your abilities, by connecting your future accomplishments to their rightful celebrations in advance.

Again, for many of us, celebrating ourselves isn't necessarily something that comes naturally. So, we have to extend grace to ourselves as we work to excel in the self-celebration learning curve. We have to train up our Celebration Factor muscles, if you will, just like we do in our workout regimens when we're looking to get stronger, faster, and/or more consistent at something. Think of it like meal prepping, but instead of popping overnight oats in the fridge, you're prepping food for the soul.

The 5-5-5 Method

One of the self-reward methods I coach my audiences and clients on that helps them to be successful in celebrating themselves is the 5-5-5 Method. In the 5-5-5 method, you start with what you know makes you feel rewarded. Make a list of those activities and categorize them into one of three categories: five minutes for the activities that only require a short amount of time, five hours for things that are more like a half-day activity, and five days for rewards that require more extended time. And I use "five" subjectively, but the gist is that whether you have a couple of minutes or half a day before jumping out of your car to put out the next fire, you can block off on your calendar a dedicated window for self-celebration and do something that makes you feel rewarded. When making time to celebrate yourself, consider whether you can carve out a few minutes, half a day, or an extended break. Do something that gets you out of the fray of the cycle you live in every day. Think of rewards that break it up and excite, relax, or satiate you.

When you create your list ahead of time and intentionally include activities that truly resonate with you, ones that feel authentic and rewarding rather than trendy or forced, you ensure your self-celebration aligns with your values and brings genuine joy. By tailoring your rewards to what genuinely fulfills you, you set the stage for meaningful, consistent self-recognition that feels sincere and empowering.

Another awesome way to develop your 5-5-5 rewards list is to ask other people what activities make them feel celebrated and rewarded. You might not naturally think of ways to celebrate, or your brain may be all tapped out from thinking about all the things, and that's okay. You do not have to reinvent the wheel here. You don't have to create methods of reward and self-celebration from scratch. Ask other people. Reach out to trusted people in your network, trusted advisors, friends, and people you see celebrating themselves regularly. What do they do? Snatch some ideas from other people. Take note of the things they share that are meaningful and have intrinsic value for you.

Selecting rewards with intrinsic value is vital. Otherwise, you may miss out on the full benefits of this cheat code. For instance, I have a girlfriend who loves designer purses and shoes, which is one way she rewards herself. I, on the other hand, am not a person who places a lot of value on purses and shoes, and that would not necessarily make me feel rewarded, so that's not going to be a meaningful way for me to celebrate myself. When we think about meaning and giving something meaning, we go inside and figure out what has intrinsic value to us. The effects of meaning-fully rewarding ourselves lasts longer, and those things stick with us. If we're doing things that make us feel something, remember, we're going for *feeling* accomplished, not just *being* accomplished, we are much more successful at repeating the behaviors that lead to our wins, which gives us even more reason to celebrate.

We have to build up the neurological network and muscle memory that allows us to do the things that make us success-ful at self-celebration. Keep in mind, we're not always going to feel like rewarding ourselves, just like we don't always feel like going to the gym. We know working out is good for us. We know it's good to move our bodies, but we might not always feel like it in the moment. However, suppose we've spent time building up that muscle memory in our bodies and our minds and filling our emotional state with dopamine that comes from celebrating ourselves. It becomes embedded in who we are. So, now we're celebrating ourselves without even having to think about it; it's just a natural response to doing something we're proud of. We reward ourselves in some way. That repetition leads to self-celebration and acknowledgment simply becoming a part of who we are. We've now established a pattern of behavior that we can start to connect the dots on. We've established that this is just what we do, and it has become known about us. Now other people are celebrating us too, by joining our parade!

I'm a big fan of mommy staycations. It's one of my all-time favorite activities on my 5-5-5 rewards list. I'll pick two days to check myself into a hotel in town where it's just me, myself, and I. I plan them regularly, at least once a quarter, and talk about them often. Everyone knows Lakila loves a good mommy staycay. Once my husband, Eric, realized, "Oh, this is really her thing," and that it brought me so much restorative joy, he joined my parade by sending my favorite treats to my room by grocery delivery service or giving me a new fluffy robe and fuzzy slippers for my stays. My favorite way he contributed to my parade was by meeting me out for lunch during one of my staycays. We had a fantastic time, and in the end, he made sure I knew how proud he was of me for taking the time I needed to recharge and how much he appreciated my commitment to prioritizing and celebrating myself. Then, he headed back home to relieve our nanny and take care of our little one. I, on the other hand, returned to my hotel to complete my mommy two-day alone time retreat. Eric's words of affirmation and genuine support made it easy for me to take the "me time" I needed to show up as the most well-cared-for version of myself. If I harbored any guilt about stepping away, his words of encouragement and acts of support would have helped alleviate it. I don't harbor a single ounce of guilt, by the way. I believe self-care is dynamically selfless, but it's still extremely reassuring to know my husband and best friend, the leader of my Support Squad, is all about my "Me Parade."

When you lead your parade with that kind of energy, people want to get in on it, and their support also adds to your ability and motivation to continue to acknowledge yourself and do the things that make you feel celebrated. Now, you're more prone to run your life in a state of fulfillment, a state of fulfillment that attracts and resonates with fulfilling actions, with fulfilling people, with fulfilling opportunities, with fulfilling resources; those things start to become a part of your orbit. They become a part of your sphere of impact and within your reach, and they become tangible to you. And it's all because you resonate at that level of personal fulfillment. You're attracting more fulfilling opportunities, experiences, people, and so on and so forth. It becomes a cycle of fulfillment that you fuel with consistency in celebrating and acknowledging yourself.

The Main Thing

Here's the main thing about the main thing: Celebrating yourself isn't just an occasional luxury, it's a vital practice for sustaining fulfillment, protecting your peace, and amplifying your achievements. Pre-planning your parade ensures that self-celebration becomes an intentional habit rather than an afterthought. By dedicating time and creating rituals that truly resonate with you, you set the stage for lasting fulfillment, self-appreciation, and a life that attracts more opportunities, resources, and meaningful connections. Lead your parade confidently and consistently, and watch how your pre-planning sets the stage for dancing your way through every perfectly good party!

Takeaways:

1. **Plan to dance at your "perfectly good" party.** Intentional celebration creates a cycle of fulfillment. Planning your celebrations in advance establishes a self-recognition habit, amplifying your joy and achievements, as well as reinforcing the behaviors that lead to regular wins and further celebrations.

2. **Develop a 5-5-5 Rewards Method list.** Choose celebration activities that align with your values and bring genuine joy, things you can do for yourself in five minutes, five hours, or over five days.

3. **Prepare for human nature and hiccups.** Planning your celebrations ahead of time removes decision-making fatigue in the moment and ensures your wins don't go unnoticed. Remember, even good change can feel daunting. Regular practice allows pre-planning your parade to become your default behavior.

4. **Fulfillment attracts fulfillment.** Celebrating yourself regularly aligns your energy with opportunities, people, and resources that resonate with your sense of personal joy and success.

Cheat Code Seven: Rest Your Bones

"The benefit of well-rested bones is a well-rested brain."—LJB

As a society, we are predominately functioning in a constant state of mental and physical exhaustion, driven largely by a need to attain more. I once had a dear friend, Cadence, who ran a very successful digital marketing agency, tell me that she and her husband often bickered about how much sleep she didn't get each night. He could see her pace was unsustainable. But she told me, "Lakila, I don't understand why he's giving me such a hard time. I can't make billions in my sleep." I said, "Sis, I gotta pause you right there... Getting sleep could very well be the key to unlocking your billions." Let me explain.

Our "functional zombie" level of exhaustion has us on such autopilot that some of our deepest energetic fields aren't being tapped into or utilized. The magnitude of our greatest divinity, creativity, and humanity lies within levels of our being accessible only when we're well-rested. This is where we begin to tap into our abilities to attain true wealth: wealth in meaningful relationships; wealth in physical and mental health; and, yes, wealth in our bank accounts.

Most importantly, you attain wealth in the form of your definition of fulfillment in life. Where money comes and goes, and even happiness can be fleeting, your fulfillment as a steady state of satiety independent of outside circumstances can be more easily accessed when you're rested. Ironically, in a world gone bananas with grind culture, you've probably been too tired to notice. The seventh and final cheat code has easily become one of my favorites, especially as I've entered the Motherhood season of my life. Rest Your Bones. By that, I mean taking time to turn it all off and literally rest. Me, myself personally, I've never met a nap I didn't love. And what better way to celebrate yourself? Siesta me, please!

The world is moving at frantic speeds; a breakneck pace has been established as the standard for our lives. Nothing turns off. We have twenty-four-hour access to everything: the news, text messages, emails, Netflix, meetings, calendars, baby monitors, AI and the list goes on, no wonder we're all out here "busy brain-did" and overwhelmed. But society adopting a frantic pace doesn't change the fact that our bodies, brains, and souls require rest to function optimally. And I mean real rest. Taking long weekend or a one-week vacation and then immediately returning to chaos does little to fulfill your natural need for downtime and recharging. We've just become so accustomed to living on the go, insufficiently rested, that we overcompensate or push through, making claims of needing only a couple hours of sleep to function.

We often forego rest at the expense of our mental, physical, and emotional well-being. Even as highly accomplished women, imagine how much more enjoyable and productive our lives could be if we weren't committed to lifestyles that glorify grind culture and the idea of "sleeping when we're dead." Research shows that adults who sleep less than six hours a night are 40 percent less productive, struggling with impaired memory, decision-making, and problem-solving. Chronic sleep deprivation also increases the risk of heart disease, diabetes, obesity, and mental health challenges like anxiety and depression. The CDC even classifies insufficient sleep as a public health epidemic. Yes, moments of intense focus and effort are inevitable, but extreme sleep deprivation was never meant to be a long-term strategy. Sleep isn't just rest, it's solace in tough times. It's a breeding ground for creativity. It's the foundation of good health. It's the charging port for our energetic completeness.

There's a price to pay when we adopt a lifestyle of being rest-deprived. It's our mental health and physical well-being that are left to foot the bill. Research backs this up. The National Sleep Foundation reports that adults need seven to nine hours of sleep per night for optimal health, yet over one-third of Americans routinely get less than six hours. On a biological level, insufficient sleep disrupts the brain's prefrontal cortex, which governs decision-making and emotional regulation, leaving us less equipped to manage the complexities of our lives. Economically, a study by Rand Corporation estimates that the U.S. economy loses approximately $411 billion annually due to sleep-related productivity declines. But there's a flipside to embrace. There's a lot to gain and an often-overlooked ROI that we can link to operating in a predominantly well-rested state.

It's clear: our grind-obsessed culture isn't helping us; it's actively hindering our ability to create meaningful wealth and fulfillment. Rest isn't just restorative; it's transformative and might be the missing ingredient for the life you're striving to build.

Naps and Whatnot

So that we're clear, I'm literally encouraging you to take naps, get in bed earlier, sleep in later, and create space to snooze. However, this cheat code can also be accessed through other means of rest, such as intentional pausing. While intentional pausing includes actual sleep, it also includes sitting still, quiet time, active meditation, zoning out, taking restorative vacations, getting massages, doing a task super-duper slow, daydreaming, sound bathing, and so on. Creating ways and time to still the mind to ponder and just be, or not to ponder at all and just be, is essential to effectively reap the benefits of celebratory self-care. You need only give yourself permission. Tell yourself that you deserve rest in any of its many variations and forms, and rest will Sho' Nuff become a part of your reality.

Rock Rest Like a Badge of Honor

Say it with me; rest is productive. Rest is my coolest friend. I am deserving of the deep embrace of rest. It's time to shift the narratives around rest as lazy and unproductive and speak about rest as our badge of honor. "Sneaking in a nap" makes it sound like you're up to no good. Reframing rest in a nontoxic manner encourages us all to proudly proclaim that we're staying well rested. To do that, we must start by connecting our rest practices to how rest is serving us. Resting your bones is a critical part of the Celebration Factor. It's truly a gift to slow down and intentionally observe our moments. We should give our brains some time offline and allow our thoughts to wander freely, led only by what moves us or strikes our curiosity.

Rest can be celebratory when we approach it with intention and gratitude. For example:

1. **Rest as Reflection:** Use rest as an opportunity to reflect on recent accomplishments. Whether reclining in a cozy chair with a warm drink or lying on a blanket in the park, acknowledge and appreciate how far you've come. Reflection during rest allows you to connect with your wins and savor them emotionally.

2. **Rest as Ritual:** Create rest rituals that feel luxurious and celebratory, light candles, put on your favorite music, and indulge in a long bath or guided meditation. Celebrate yourself by creating a special environment acknowledging your humanity, including hard work and achievements, but also your uniqueness and inner light.

3. **Rest as Reward:** Tie moments of rest into your 5-5-5 Reward Method. No matter how big or small an accomplishment, treat yourself to a nap without guilt or an entire day of doing nothing but lounging in your favorite pajamas. Make rest a tangible acknowledgment of your success. Sidenote: Don't allow a lack of feeling accomplished keep you from resting.

4. **Rest as Exploration:** Allow your rest time to double as a gateway to creative exploration. Rest can spark innovation and problem-solving, as our minds often make new connections when they're not actively focused on a task. Take a walk without a destination, lie in a hammock, hide in a closet so your kids can't find you, or journal freely, do what you need to do to let your thoughts flow. Let rest be a playground for your imagination.

5. **Rest as Connection:** Celebrate rest with others by organizing low-energy but high-reward gatherings. Invite friends over for a laid-back movie night, or plan a family day of board games and cozy blankets. Participate in sound baths. Start a Nap Challenge. Instead of ten thousand steps, set a goal of "ten thousand winks." Shared rest can be deeply restorative and affirming.

When you view rest as an act of celebration, you give yourself permission to embrace it unapologetically. You acknowledge that you are worthy of restoration and that rest is not just a pause but a powerful tool for rejuvenation, creativity, and fulfillment. It's a practice that reminds us that our best selves emerge not from relentless grinding but from a harmonious balance of effort and renewal. Rest is how we refuel, reignite, and reconnect with the essence of who we are beyond our résumés and titles.

Skip the Scrolling

And as tempting as it may be, I urge you to resist the pull of social media during your downtime. Listen, I love a good laugh at a funny meme or post as much as the next person, but let's keep it real, social media is a trap. It's engineered to hijack your attention, keeping you endlessly scrolling, consuming, and comparing. And if we're really being honest, how often do you really come out of a scrolling session feeling refreshed? Probably never.

Social media highlight reels are just that, highlights. They're someone else's best moments, often filtered and edited to perfection. Comparing your raw, unfiltered life to their reel can leave you questioning your wins, doubting your journey, and feeling like you're somehow behind. It's a setup, Ladies. Scrolling doesn't just waste time; it drains your energy and pulls you away from the very things that could be restoring you.

So, instead of scrolling, make a deliberate choice to pour into yourself. Use that downtime to journal your wins, catch up on a book that sparks joy or ideas, meditate, or simply sit in stillness. Go outside, feel the sun on your skin, and remind yourself of the beauty and abundance in your own world. These moments are about you, celebrating your wins, nurturing your soul, and giving your brain a break from all the noise.

By skipping the scrolling, you reclaim something invaluable: your time and energy. Instead of getting caught in someone else's story, you can live fully in your own. Want to improve your rest hygiene? One of the first places I look to clean up is time spent on socials and/or staring at screens.

The Main Thing

Here's the main thing about the main thing: Understanding that you don't have to do anything special to deserve rest is critical. The human body requires downtime to recharge, regenerate, and function properly. Rest for rest's sake is enough. Taking your brain and body offline allows you to recover and operate at your best. Studies show that adequate rest improves memory, enhances creativity, and increases productivity by up to 20 percent. Chronic sleep deprivation, on the other hand, is linked to reduced cognitive function, increased stress, and even long-term health issues like heart disease. Prioritizing rest is not just about avoiding burnout; it's about optimizing your ability to thrive.

When you give yourself permission to rest, you reclaim your energy and capacity for success and true fulfillment. Make rest nonnegotiable and celebrate it as an act of self-care that fuels every other area of your life. Remember, rest is productive, restorative, and a portal to the best version of who we are at our core.

Takeaways:

1. **Your bones need resting.** Rest is essential for physical, mental, and emotional well-being. It's not a luxury but a human necessity. Your bones will thank you.

2. **Tap in with rest.** Prioritizing downtime improves our ability to unlock levels of our creativity, divinity, and humanity that rely on restoration.

3. **Grind culture is a recipe for burnout.** Though there are times when we need moments of intense focus, chronic sleep deprivation negatively impacts your health, increasing stress and the risk of serious conditions like heart disease. Even when your mission is greater than you, rest amplifies your impact.

4. **Rest is many things.** Rest is ritual, reflection, reward, exploration, and connection to ourselves and others. Through rest, we gain so much more than rest.

5. **Glorify rest.** Treat your acts of rest as a badge of honor by centering rest as a foundational part of your success and happiness.

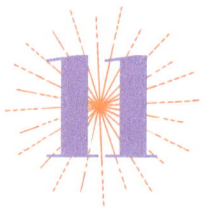

Jackie Taught Me

"I've had a real good time.", Jacqueline Renee Bowens (My mom)

"We're taking Ma to the beach!" That was the announcement I made to my husband in the middle of the night. Over the past few months since my mother had been placed on home hospice, I'd been coming up with all kinds of ways to put a smile on her face: buying cute, comfy lounge clothes in fun colors, taking her on drives through her childhood neighborhood in Savoy Heights and listening to all of her funny stories, and arranging for "Zoom Parties" with her favorite family members so she could receive her flowers while she could still smell them.

We were in what would become her final stages of hospice care, and my focus had shifted from trying everything energetically and medically possible to reverse her cancer to doing everything energetically that I could to bring as much life and light to the time she had left, *we* had left. Her mobility had become a challenge, but something in my spirit said, "She needs the beach...

We need the beach." So, as I made my proclamation in the middle of the night, my half-asleep husband looked at me, five-months pregnant and so determined, and said, "To the beach we go. Let's do it!"

A week later, Ma, Kamille, Eric, and I were packed into an SUV and on the road to a beachfront rental on Topsail Island, about a two-hour drive from my hometown in Fayetteville, North Carolina where my mother resided and Kamille and I had grown up. On the drive, we sang songs and ate road snacks. I'd long since stopped being the Food Patrol, monitoring every bite my mom took and often vetoing what I deemed unhealthy choices. Now, I didn't stop her from munching on whatever her heart desired. Her appetite had largely waned, but she enjoyed the unrestricted treats nonetheless. When we pulled up to our ocean view condo for the weekend, we discovered that our assigned unit provided stairs-only access. My mom looked disappointed. At this point, she'd lost most of her strength and weighed but a fraction of the full-bodied woman she used to be, resulting in her mobility being extremely limited. "How will I get up there?" she asked, gazing out of the truck window at what I'm sure looked like a zillion stairs. Eric, with one foot already out of the vehicle, flashed a reassuring smile and said, "I'm gonna carry you, Ma." A look of relief washed over her face as she replied, "Then I know I'm in good hands." And so it went. Gentle as if he were picking up our soon-to-be-born son, Eric lifted my mom from her seat and carried her up the stairs cradled carefully in his strong arms.

Once inside, we made sure my mom had the room facing the ocean and the best view in the house. Over the course of the weekend, we soaked up the warm ocean air, binged our favorite shows all night, talked, laughed, snacked, and indulged in the quiet solitude we'd found in our little beach cove hide away. It was one of those weekends where time moves slowly, each moment stands still, and it feels like nothing and no one else exists other than your present company. On our final morning, I sat in bed with Mom listening to the waves rhythmically washing upon the shore down below. We held hands, and she said to me "You know, Kila, even with everything that's gone on, I've had a real good time." My heart swelled inside my chest. Her words settled my restless soul. I knew that was her way of telling me my mission to bring love and light to her journey had been accomplished.

Exactly one month later, my mother made her peaceful transition from this Earth. As I went about the business of laying her to rest, eventually birthing my son, Zaire, navigating postpartum while learning to be a mother, prioritizing healing and seeking joy, her words played over and over in my head. "I've had a real good time." More than anything, those words reinforced the necessity of celebratory self-care in my life and in the work I've been called to do as a speaker and company founder. We don't always control the circumstances in which we find ourselves. Life can absolutely throw us some curve balls, sucker punches, and straight up roundhouse kicks to the face. We can choose to see these moments as devastating and debilitating, or we can choose to embrace them as divine disruptions meant to ultimately serve in our favor. I chose the latter.

Even in navigating the grief of my Mother's physical absence, I've elected thoughts and actions steeped in self-care and self-celebration to chart my course. For me, the Sho' Nuff Principle is a living, breathing, ever-evolving ethos woven into the fabric of my life that guides and amplifies the brilliance of my existence.

Professionally and personally applicable, the cheat codes that lay the foundation for the principle of determining one's own well-cared-for and well-celebrated reality have been proven game changers time and time again for the legions of women I've worked with and who've accepted them as their most trusted asset in their call to greatness. And for that, without a doubt, I have my mother to thank. At every stage of my life and through the end of her own, she showed me how to really have a good time!

Ain't No Party Like a Sho' Nuff Party, 'Cause a Sho' Nuff Party Don't Stop

So now that we're nearing the wrap-up of our journey into the practical magnificence of the Sho' Nuff Principle, let me ask you: Did you have a real good time? Did you find moments along the way where you wanted to test out that two-step, and maybe even throw in a little shoulder shimmy? Perhaps you felt the urge to pause and gather up your Support Squad to discuss what you read, over wine or sparkling cider of course. Bonus points if after reading Cheat Code Seven: Rest Your Bones, you went and took a nap! I have no doubt the answer to these questions, and so many more, is now a resounding "YASSSSS!"

If you felt any inkling of inspiration, rejuvenation, or empowerment, then consider this your invitation to make celebratory self-care a way of life, 'cause a Sho' Nuff Party don't stop. The seven cheat codes I've shared with you in the pages of this book are your all-access pass to transform how you navigate your world. They're a blueprint, empowering you to honor your brilliance and prioritize your well-being unapologetically, without compromise, in celebratory fashion. Sho' Nuff!

FINAL THOUGHTS

"Teach a woman to fish, and the village will eat for generations to come."—LJB

What's Next for You?

You've explored the cheat codes, reflected on the stories, and, I hope, seen pieces of your journey on these pages. Now it's your turn. Take a moment to reflect: Which cheat code resonated with you the most? Was it the call to practice self-compassion and silence your inner critic? The reminder to pause and ground yourself in the present through mindfulness? Perhaps it was the challenge to brag more and celebrate yourself unapologetically. Wherever you felt the strongest pull, that's your starting point. Where do you see opportunities to grow, celebrate, or shift your focus? This is the beginning of your next chapter, a life lived fully, unapologetically, and joyfully.

This book is your foundation, but transformation lies in your hands. So, I invite you to think deeply: What's next for you? Whatever speaks to you most, trust that it's the right place to begin, and I've got your back.

Let Me Be Part of Your Journey

If you're wondering how to keep the party going and turn what you've learned into a lasting transformation, you don't have to figure it out alone. This is where I can help. Whether it's through speaking engagements that energize and inspire your teams, workshops for your organization, or coaching sessions to support your personal growth, I'm here to guide you. Together, we can take what you've started here and amplify it.

So, what's next for you? That's entirely up to you! Just know you have someone here to help in any way needed. Reach out and let's take the next step together. I promise, we'll make it a two-step.

lakila@lakilabowden.com
www.lakilabowden.com

ACKNOWLEDGEMENTS

First, it's my greatest joy to give thanks to my magnificent husband, Eric Bowden, whose love and presence in my life is the physical manifestation of the very essence of The Sho' Nuff Principle in action. I thank you, Handsome, for your gifts of being wise beyond your years and effortlessly cool. Then I must, of course, thank the little love of my life, Zaire Aasir, my Sun. You are my greatest creation and the opportunity to experience motherhood as your mother affirms my soul's existence beyond what the mind can fathom. Next, my awe-inspiring almost twin sister, Kamille Richardson. Thank you for reading this manuscript from start to finish, from cover to cover, from its infancy and through every iteration thereafter. Your always encouraging feedback, precise insights, and hilarious takes made every rewrite a ridiculously good time! More contract snacks to come!

To my dear beautiful mother, Jacqueline Renee Bowens. I had no clue we were writing the chapters to my book in your final year earth side. Thank you, Ma, for your love in this life, for your guidance that transcends this realm and remains present by my side every single day, and for making sure we had so much fun growing up. It really was a good time.

To my dad, G. Milton Richardson. Thank you for teaching me to always shoot my shot and for making me into the bravest woman I could be. You've always known how to motivate me with gentle words, fierce protection, and unwavering belief in what I can do.

To the remainder of my village, thank you for being a part of my Squad and for your support, whether direct or indirect, in bringing this work forth in such a meaningful way. To be consistently surrounded by such genuine love and positive energy is how I know I'm doing it right!

Sho' Nuff,
Lakila

ABOUT THE AUTHOR

Dr. Lakila Bowden, Speaker, Author, and Founder

Dr. Lakila Bowden is the charismatic voice high-achieving women didn't know they were missing. A visionary speaker, company founder, and unapologetic rest advocate, she's the COO of iSee Technologies and author of The Sho' Nuff Principle: A High Achieving Woman's Guide to Self-Care, Self-Promotion, & Self-Celebration.

After a thriving executive career in Fortune 500 companies like GE and DaVita, and retiring from corporate America at just 37, Dr. Bowden's charted a bold path that's led to her becoming a trusted voice on stage for powerhouse organizations like The Walt Disney Company, Kraft Heinz, Verizon, and JP Morgan.

Lakila embraces a multi-hyphenate lifestyle which aligns with her personal ethos to operate in flow vs force in wealth creation and living life in celebratory fashion.

As a proud North Carolina A&T Aggie Alum, her academic credentials, including an MBA from Emory University and an honorary doctorate in Humanitarianism, bolster her practical strategies for balancing demanding careers with personal well-being.

She resides in the Atlanta area, enjoying the adventures of life with her remarkable husband, Eric, and their brilliant and kind son, Zaire Aasir.

www.ingramcontent.com/pod-product-compliance
Lightning Source LLC
Chambersburg PA
CBHW061650120626
46550CB00003B/888